Stella Atterbury was an interested but dilettante cook until she first cooked for her family of four just after the War. A few years later she and her husband bought an old manor house in Somerset which they converted into a country-house hotel. This in due course was listed in the A.A. and R.A.C. handbooks and recommended in the *Good Food Guide*. It was while cooking for her hotel that the author evolved many culinary ideas with the view of obtaining the best possible results with the expenditure of the least possible time and effort. These are given in her books *Never Too Late, Cook Ahead, Waste Not, Want Not* and *The Smallest Freezers*.

On retirement Stella Atterbury and her husband lived in a Sussex village where the Slow Cooking Method was practised with enthusiasm, and it was found as useful for two as it had been for unpredictable numbers. Even with a ménage of one, the Method proved equally valuable both for routine meals and entertaining – especially so when a slow-cooking electric casserole is also used and cooked dishes can be stored in a freezer. Stella Atterbury died in 1977.

Leave it to Cook

THE SLOW COOKING METHOD

Stella Atterbury

Penguin Books

Penguin Books Ltd, Harmondsworth, Middlesex, England
Penguin Books, 625 Madison Avenue, New York,
New York 10022, U.S.A.
Penguin Books Australia Ltd, Ringwood, Victoria, Australia
Penguin Books Canada Ltd, 2801 John Street, Markham,
Ontario, Canada L3R 1B4
Penguin Books (N.Z.) Ltd, 182–190 Wairau Road, Auckland 10,
New Zealand

First published 1968
Reprinted 1969, 1971, 1972, 1973, 1975, 1976
Reprinted with revisions 1977
Reprinted 1977
Reprinted with revisions 1978
Reprinted 1978

Made and printed in Great Britain by
Hazell Watson & Viney Ltd, Aylesbury, Bucks
Set in Linotype Juliana

To My Husband

Contents

8 Contents

Author's Foreword

'The slower the cooking the better the result' can be said of a number of foods. These, when left in a very cool oven for about eight hours or longer, will not only cook to perfection, but will also retain the natural juices and flavours which are often lost when food is cooked at a higher temperature. In addition this slow method gives the cook the opportunity and satisfaction of being away from the kitchen while good meals are cooking.

If the oven is filled to capacity, there is an obvious saving of time, and, in the case of gas and electricity, expense too.

Dishes for weeks or months ahead can be cooked at one session, provided a refrigerator or freezer is available for storage.

The period in which the oven takes over the cooking is a matter of convenience. For instance, when cooking for our country hotel, as described in my book *Never Too Late*, I found it a godsend to lighten my day's burden by cooking as many dishes as possible during the night. Now, in my retirement, the pattern has changed. Life being comparatively leisurely, my oven or slow-cooking electric casserole more often cooks for me throughout the day; thus, while gardening or pursuing other activities, I can look forward to a nice hot carefree evening meal.

Though for many years an enthusiastic follower of the Slow Cooking Method, I felt I should not embark on this book before obtaining the views and findings of others regarding cookers, food preferences, meal times and households, all differing considerably from my own. That is why I enlisted the help of a few friends and neighbours to form a Slow Cooking working party. We met regularly for six months, and these are our unanimous conclusions:

The Slow Cooking Method can be adapted to most cookers and will prove beneficial to housewives catering for small or large families of all ages, but will be especially valuable to those who are away from home during the day.

We have tried out the given recipes and now sincerely hope that others will also enjoy cooking while they sleep, work or play.

Acknowledgements

Many have helped, both consciously and unconsciously, towards the writing of this book. Ruth Martin, with her technical and literary advice – Ailsa Crawley, B.SC., A.R.I.C., who is always at hand to elucidate scientific problems – and the willing working party: Margaret Biker, Jean Godfrey, Freda King, Audrey Pullen and June Thompson, who tested my recipes in their own kitchens and gave me their unbiased views on the Slow Cooking Method. My cordial thanks to them all. It would be invidious to select only a few from the innumerable friends, acquaintances and cookery writers who, for nearly half a century, have added to my culinary knowledge. To them also I offer my gratitude.

S.A.

The Slow Cooking Method

As I have said in my Foreword, the Slow Cooking Method saves energy and working time in the kitchen – especially when some of the dishes, cooked for future meals, are stored in the refrigerator or freezer. Foods that respond to this method are invariably perfectly cooked because they are not allowed to simmer, boil or reach a heat that dries up the natural juices and lets the flavour deteriorate.

The Slow Cooking Method can be practised in the ovens of electric and gas cookers, the simmering ovens of Aga, Esse and some Rayburn cookers, and in slow-cooking electric casseroles. See *Notes on Electric Casseroles*, pages 22 to 25, also pages 12, 13, 14 and 17.

The heat of electric and gas ovens at their lowest settings is not likely to be lower than 145° F. (63° C.), the heat at which most bacteria begin to die. The higher the temperature the more quickly they die. The ideal temperature for ultra-slow cooking is over 180° F. (82° C.) and under 200° F. (93° C.) which is the equivalent of gas mark S* or *low*. Some cookers, however, are not marked lower than 200° F. (93° C.) or mark ¼ which is a little too hot. Still, these cookers will often function at a slightly lower temperature. In any case – unless an oven is designed for that purpose – before slow cooking can be fully enjoyed, a spell of trial and error will be necessary so that the cook, her cooker and the method

*Gas cookers with an S setting are especially designed by Flavel for the Slow Cooking Method.

can adjust themselves to each other. The first time it is tried, set the oven just over 180° F. (82° C.) or gas mark S or low, or, if it does not register as low as that, set it as low as it will function. Put in one or two simple dishes and leave them for about eight hours.

If after that time the food is cooked to perfection, you have established the right setting for your slow cooking.

If the food is undercooked, give it a little longer at a slightly higher temperature, and next time you experiment, use a fractionally higher setting in the first place.

If, on the other hand, your first setting proves too hot for slow cooking, the food will have simmered and be somewhat overcooked. Next time, if possible, try a lower setting, otherwise you must follow Choice 2 given below.

However, as long as food is left in a very cool oven it will never be burnt or ruined, the reason being that, once food reaches the temperature of the oven in which it has been placed, it cannot get any hotter. Food left in an oven perfectly adjusted to slow cooking may be cooked well before the eight hours are up, but will come to no harm if left for the full time. This gives owners of ovens amenable to the Slow Cooking Method or those with electric casseroles a choice:

Choice 1 Suitable for day or night cooking where the food is left to be cooked for eight hours or longer.

Choice 2 Suitable for day cooking only where the food needs to be inspected periodically after the first 4–6 hours' cooking and removed if already cooked.

There are some foods, such as fish and eggs, that will be cooked in 1–5 hours. These can be found in the Index under *Dishes Cooked for 1–5 Hours* and on pages 31 to 38 and 130 to 132.

Our circumstances and ways of living decide whether slow cooking takes place during the day or night. Fortunately, most slowly cooked dishes can be reheated without deterioration. Beside those recipes which do suffer from reheating I have added a warning: *Day cooking only. Do not reheat.* Also, conveniently, many dishes can be prepared well in advance of cooking, which obviates the unpopular early morning preparation of dishes to be cooked throughout that day.

The fear of greatly increased fuel bills is most people's re-action to ultra-slow cooking. This is not justified provided as many dishes as possible are cooked at the same time. In fact there may be a small saving of cost – certainly a considerable saving of time and energy with the pleasure of finding, after hours of unsupervised cooking, a nice hot meal for immediate consumption, together with a selection of dishes for the weeks ahead. Slow-cooking electric casseroles definitely reduce costs.

Careful stacking is vital if your oven is to accommodate the greatest variety of dishes, each in its favoured position. The temperature of ovens (except fan heated), whatever the set-ting, varies slightly according to the shelf position. The hottest place in all ovens is the top shelf. The coolest place in all gas and some electric ovens is the bottom shelf, though in other electric ovens it is the middle shelf. The oven floor of electric cookers can be used for slow cooking but is usually not hot enough in gas cookers. Sample oven loads are given on pages 18 and 19.

An additional advantage of slow cooking is the easing of that horrid chore – oven cleaning. Not only is fat-splashing eliminated, but any deposits on the oven lining are more easily removed.

The slow-cooking recipes in this book are intended to sup-plement, not supplant, favourite recipes already in daily use. However, it is surprising how many types of food benefit from or adapt to this method.

FOODS THAT BENEFIT FROM
ULTRA-SLOW COOKING

Meat, Poultry and Game come first in this category led by casseroled dishes. These surpass themselves when cooked in the medium or hottest position of a very cool oven or in an electric casserole. Methods of roasting meat very slowly with excellent results are explained on pages 75 to 78.

Egg* and Milk Dishes, the custard type, cooked uncovered in a medium oven position, never burn or curdle and need not be stood in water. For cooking in an electric casserole see page 24.

Cereal and Milk Dishes, sweet and savoury. These, when cooked covered in the hottest position of an ultra-slow oven or in an electric casserole, could not be creamier. All the cream remains in the dish; it is not dissipated in the skin.

Stewed Fruits. Cook covered in medium or cooler oven position or in an electric casserole with sweetening but very little, if any, liquid. These retain the maximum flavour and never mush.

Dried Fruits. Cook covered in medium or hot oven position or in an electric casserole with plenty of liquid. Very little, if any, sweetening is needed.

Jams and Preserves – pages 138 to 146.

Pulses – pages 104 to 105.

Pin-head Oatmeal for making real Scotch porridge – page 136.

* Do not use duck's eggs in any slowly cooked dishes. These eggs should always be cooked at a high temperature to avoid risk of salmonella poisoning.

FOODS THAT ADAPT THEMSELVES TO ULTRA-SLOW COOKING

These foods are no better cooked by this method, but are as good as when cooked normally. They add variety to slow cooking and are particularly useful to people away from home all day.

Egg, Milk and Bread Dishes. Sweet or savoury. Cook uncovered in medium or hot oven position. For cooking in an electric casserole, see page 24.

Root and other vegetables – pages 97 to 104.

Rice – pages 126 to 130.

FOOD THAT BENEFITS FROM A SHORTER PERIOD OF ULTRA-SLOW COOKING

Fish and some egg dishes come under this heading. All fish recipes that are cooked in the oven are delicious when subjected to this low temperature. They will, however, be cooked in 1 to 2 hours, though come to no harm when left in the oven for considerably longer. See pages 31 to 38 and 130 to 132.

PRE-COOKING PREPARATION

The time needed to cook meals is all-important to busy people; but when using the Slow Cooking Method, it is only the preparation time that must be reckoned, not the many hours the dishes cook in the oven or electric casserole.

Most slowly cooked dishes can be prepared in advance, stored and cooked as convenient. Those that must be cooked as soon as they are prepared are specified in the recipes. Otherwise, for day cooking, dishes can be prepared the evening before and stored overnight in a refrigerator; for night cooking, they can be prepared during the day. Chilling dishes before cooking is an advantage if the oven is a little on the hot side.

STORAGE AND REHEATING

When the oven is filled with a variety of dishes, not all can be served as soon as they are cooked. Some that can be served cold or do not suffer from reheating, after rapid cooling, can be stored for up to three days in the refrigerator or up to three to four months in the freezer.

Dishes reheated from the refrigerator must go directly into a hot oven or a pan over gentle direct heat.

Dishes reheated from the freezer can either be thawed in the refrigerator and reheated as above or, while still frozen, placed in a cold oven which is then switched to 400° F., 200° C. or gas mark 6, or can be placed in a pan over gentle direct heat.

Whichever way dishes are heated, they must be really hot – meat and poultry casseroles brought to simmering – and must be served immediately. Never reheat meat more than once.

SLOW COOKING UTENSILS

Cooks rarely possess all the utensils they consider they need, and those who practise slow cooking certainly do need oven dishes and casseroles of all shapes and sizes. The most valuable of these is the flame-proof variety – the type that can come out of a refrigerator onto a gas jet, an electric hot-plate, or into an oven, and, after all that, look attractive on the dining table. Some are made of cast iron covered with coloured vitreous enamel – lighter, somewhat cheaper and very pleasant to use are the Pyrosil saucepans – frying pans-cum-casseroles – with a useful, detachable, interchangeable handle.

Cheaper enamelware, however, is a more economical solution to the utensil problem. This can usually be bought at Woolworths. It may already be in your kitchen cupboard. Excellent small casseroles can be improvised with enamel basins covered with 7″ (17 cm) or 8″ (20 cm) glass or enamel plates, or with just aluminium foil. Laminated foil dishes intended for freezing can also be used for slow cooking. They can be placed over gentle direct heat for the preliminary cooking of ingredients such as bacon or onions. These containers are useful as dishes to be stored, also for using in electric casseroles. When a larger casserole is needed, self-basting roasters are the answer. These should last for years, even if placed over direct heat for a short spell of frying or boiling before entering a cool oven. Of course earthenware basins can also act as casseroles but these cannot be placed over direct heat. When recipes state that food should be covered with a tightly fitting lid, a piece of foil fixed over the utensil under the lid will rectify a bad fit. Composition handles come to no harm in an ultra-slow oven.

A slow-cooking electric casserole is both a utensil and a cooker for the Slow Cooking Method. It is especially useful for small families or when only one slowly cooked dish is required. It uses very little electricity, in fact no more than a light bulb.

Gadgets are fascinating but not indispensable, with the exception of a meat thermometer. Without one of these, slow roasting cannot be perfect every time.

Sample Oven Loads

The following suggested oven loads are only intended to offer some examples of dishes that can be cooked during one slow-cooking session. The sizes of ovens and containers obviously vary considerably and not everyone will be able to accommodate all the given dishes. On the other hand, if there is room to spare, another dish or a stopgap (pages 133 to 146) can be put in the oven.

The dishes chosen for the following loads, supplemented by salads, freshly cooked vegetables (pages 97 and 147) and perhaps fruit and cheese, are planned to provide at least three main meals for two or three persons.

They can be cooked either by day or by night, provided that any night-cooked roasts are kept hot until the mid-day meal, unless they are to be served cold.

LOAD 1.

A joint for roasting (pages 75 to 78)
Oxtail (page 49)
Savoury Pie (page 123)

Fried Rice (page 126)
Fruit Meringue Pie (page 110)
Caramel Custard (page 107)

LOAD 2.

Veal Casserole (page 52)
Beef Creole (page 47)
Onion in Sago Sauce (page 100)
Chicken Broth (page 27)

Honey and Ginger pudding (page 119)
Orange Whip (page 114)

LOAD 3.

Hamburgers (page 80)
Irish Stew (page 53)
Pigeon Casserole (page 64)

Apricot or Fig Fiesta (page 112)
Sultana Pudding (page 116)
A Creamed Vegetable (page 98)

LOAD 4.

Roast Chicken (pages 75 to 78)
Bacon or Ham Joint (page 72)
Steak and Kidney 2 (page 41)
Chocolate Coffee Cream
    (page 108)

Apple Almond Pudding
    (page 120)
Rice Balls (page 127)
    or
Creamed Potatoes (page 104)

ECONOMY LOAD

Stuffed Breast of Lamb
    (page 78)
Economy Stew (page 54)
Ham Loaf (page 73)

Milk Pudding (page 106)
Apple Charlotte (page 120)
Onion Soup (page 29)

PARTY LOAD

Before a party, plan a load to include a selection of dishes from those give in the index under PARTY DISHES.

Weights and Measures

Metric weights and measures have come to stay and we must get used to them. The exact equivalents of our British weights and measures would be awkward and unpractical for daily use. Try to convert a recipe with the correct assumption that 1 British ounce equals 28·35 grammes! To make life easier powers that be have given us the following approximate conversions.

BRITISH		APPROX. METRIC CONVERSIONS
1 oz	=	25 g
¼ lb	=	100 g
½ lb	=	200 g
1 lb	=	400 g
2¼ lb	=	1 kg

BRITISH		APPROX. METRIC CONVERSIONS
1 teaspoon	=	5 ml
1 dessertspoon (2 teaspoons)	=	10 ml
1 tablespoon	=	15 ml
1 fluid oz	=	25 ml
¼ pint (5 fluid oz)	=	125 ml
½ pint	=	250 ml
1 pint	=	500 ml

These conversions being slightly less than their British counterparts, means that the results of converted recipes will be slightly smaller than the originals, though the relative weights and measures of the individual ingredients will be correct. It is therefore important that either the British or the approximate metric conversions should be consistently used throughout a recipe.

The spoons given in the following recipes are standard measuring spoons and should be level unless otherwise stated.

Notes on Timing for the Slow Cooking Method

It is important that pages 11 to 17, explaining the Slow Cooking Method, are carefully studied before the recipes are tried.

All the recipes, unless otherwise stated, can be cooked in an ultra-slow oven for up to eight hours or longer and most of them, though the technique is somewhat different, can also be cooked in an electric casserole. See notes that follow and consult comparable recipes in the leaflet provided with your casserole regarding specific settings and timing.

NOTES ON SLOW-COOKING ELECTRIC CASSEROLES AND ADAPTING RECIPES

These have been extremely popular in the U.S.A. for some time. Until recently, the only slow-cooking casseroles on the market in this country were the 'Tower Electric Casserole' and the same company's larger 'Slo-Cooker'. Now, while preparing this reprint, two other manufacturers offer respectively a 'Crock-Pot' and a 'Cookpot', which give would-be purchasers the choice of four attractive and efficient slow-cooking casseroles. It is hoped the following notes will help their deliberations.

Capacity. The two smaller casseroles hold approximately 3¼ or 3½ pints (1.8 or 2 litres) and are suitable for households of up to three. Larger families or those who prepare food for freezing will need one of the larger casseroles, holding approximately 5¾ or 6 pints (3.2 or 3.5 litres).

Detachable Earthenware Bowls. One of the smaller and one of the larger cookers have removable stoneware containers. These cost more than the all-in-one type and monopolize more working surface or storage space. On the other hand, they are easier to wash, cooked dishes can be crispened or browned in the oven or under the grill, and, should there be an accident, the bowl can be replaced more easily and at less cost.

Indicator Lights. One of the smaller and one of the larger casseroles are fitted with indicator lights to illuminate the switch whenever it is on – a boon to busy and perhaps forgetful cooks.

Settings. Slow-cooking casseroles have two heats: *low*, which is roughly the same as an ultra-slow oven; and *high*, which is twice as quick as *low*. This means that most of the recipes that can be 'left to cook' in the ultra-cool oven will cook as well and in about the same time in an electric casserole set at *low* and in about half the time set at *high*. There is however a problem with one of the larger casseroles. The accompanying instructions stress that all meat, poultry and fish dishes *must* be cooked on *high* for two hours before being switched to *low*. This ruling prevents those who are away during the day considering an otherwise excellent casserole. However, it is quite likely that before long the makers will adjust their 'Cookpot' to allow all-day cooking. Some foods prefer to be cooked entirely on *high* and these will be indicated in the following recipes. Some dishes, meat and poultry casseroles in particular, can be given a preliminary boost of a ¼ to ½ an hour on *high* before being switched to *low*. However long food is subjected to either setting it cannot burn or dry up – on *low* it will come to no harm if left considerably longer than the stipulated time, although on *high*, even after only a little longer cooking, it will become overcooked.

The cooking is expedited when the casserole is pre-heated. Get into the habit of switching on to *high* and heating it for up to twenty minutes while the recipe is being prepared. The food, however, still cooks beautifully with less or no pre-heating of the casserole, but will naturally take a little longer – as will the slaughter of any lurking bacteria. Cooking can also be accelerated if liquid ingredients over ¼ pint (125 ml) are first warmed, heated or brought to the boil.

Baking in the true sense – to cook by dry heat – cannot be achieved in a slow-cooking casserole as it can in an ultra-slow oven. This is partly because the confined air space round the food will be moist but mainly because the container in which the food is cooked must be stood on a rack (a jam jar lid or just crumpled foil will do) and hot water to a depth of about 1″ (2–3 cm) must be poured into the hot casserole. This is most important, as I learnt to my cost, otherwise the contact of the hot container with the dry casserole is liable to fracture the earthenware. Still, most of the recipes that bake slowly in the oven will cook satisfactorily in an electric casserole provided the above rules are followed. Any ovenware can be used – laminated foil (intended for freezing) and boilable plastic (with lids) are good, especially for custards.

Moist recipes, which include all the custard types, must be well covered with foil or a tightly fitting lid.

For *crisper or drier recipes*, do not fill containers too full. First, cover with buttered grease-proof paper, then with four or five layers of absorbent kitchen paper, and finally with foil. The cooked dish can be given a spell under the grill to help brown and crispen the top.

When meat or poultry is roasted in a slow-cooking casserole, it should first be browned all over in a frying pan and the casserole pre-heated for the full 20 minutes. Should the joint or bird have been frozen, make sure it is completely thawed before frying to avoid the risk of Salmonella food poisoning. (The 'Cookpot' instruction book bans the roasting of meat or poultry in their casserole – possibly because of the fear that cooks might disregard the complete thawing, especially of frozen birds or pork.) The meat is unwrapped and, unless very fatty, a rack is unnecessary. Grease the casserole for lean meat. Pork and chicken should be cooked throughout at *high*; other meats can be switched to *low* after the first 30 to 60 minutes.

Soups

A few slowly cooked soups are given here, as even in this day of commercial soups a good hot home-made soup is always welcome, especially on a winter night. They are also economical, so justify oven space.

Chicken Broth

Coolest oven position or electric casserole
Approx. preparation time 2 minutes
Cook as soon as prepared

This is really good and very quick to prepare. The required chicken necks, giblets, and hearts are obtainable at Sainsbury's and often at other provision stores that have a large turnover in chicken joints.

For 3 or 4 portions allow:

½ lb (200 g) chicken necks, etc.
1 tbs. (15 ml) Patna rice
1 medium onion, sliced
¾ tsp. (3.75 ml) salt
pepper to taste

either 1 tbs. (15 ml) chopped fresh parsley or 2 tsp. (10 ml) dried parsley
½–1 clove garlic, crushed in salt (optional)
12 fl. oz (300 ml) milk and water

Place all the ingredients in a stewpan or saucepan with a closely fitting lid and bring to the boil on the hob. As soon as it boils, cook in the oven or heated electric casserole.

When cooked, remove the chicken necks, etc. Their goodness is in the broth, and they are now only fit for your or your neighbour's cat.

Cream of Leek or Celery Soup

Medium or cool oven position or electric casserole
Approx. preparation time 10 minutes
For 2–3 portions allow:

1 oz (25 g) butter or margarine	2 tbs. (30 ml) flour
2 small or 1 large leek, cut into small pieces, or 4–6 sticks of celery also cut into small pieces	½ pt (250 ml) stock or water and ½ stock cube
	½ pt (250 ml) milk
	salt and pepper to taste

Melt the fat in a pan with a well-fitting lid and cook the leeks or celery for a few minutes over a gentle heat. Remove pan from stove, and with a wooden spoon stir in the flour. When well blended, gradually add the liquid, and finally the seasoning. Return pan to heat and stir until the soup thickens and begins to boil. At this point, either cook the soup or store and cook later, in which case, bring to the boil again before putting into the oven or heated electric casserole. If a thinner soup is preferred, add a little more liquid.

Split Pea Soup

Hot or medium oven position or electric casserole
Approx. preparation time 5 minutes
For 4 portions allow:

4 fl. oz (100 ml) split peas, washed and drained	¼ tsp. (1·25 ml) Worcester sauce
1 small carrot, cubed	1½ pt (750 ml) stock or 1 pt (500 ml) water and ½ pt (250 ml) milk
1 small onion, grated	
1 bay leaf	
¼–½ tsp. (1·25–2·5 ml) salt and a little pepper	½ oz (12·5 g) lean bacon, chopped (optional)

Put all the ingredients in a stewpan or saucepan with a well-fitting lid. Either bring to the boil and immediately cook in the oven or a heated electric casserole, or store and bring the soup to the boil just before slow cooking.

Onion Soup

Medium or cool oven position or electric casserole
Approx. preparation time 4 minutes
For 2 or 3 portions allow:

1 oz (25 g) butter	½ tsp. (2·5 ml) Worcester
1 large onion, finely sliced	sauce
2 tsp. (10 ml) flour	salt and pepper
a stock cube and 1 pt (500 ml)	1 slice of toasted bread per
water or 1 pt (500 ml) good	portion
stock	grated Parmesan or Cheddar
	cheese

Melt the butter in a stewpan or saucepan and fry the onion until it begins to brown. Remove pan from heat, and with a wooden spoon stir in the flour and, if used, the stock cube. Gradually add the liquids. Season to taste. Either bring to the boil, cover closely and immediately cook in the oven or a heated electric casserole, or store and bring the soup to the boil just before slow cooking.

Prior to serving, pour the hot soup into a shallow oven dish or into individual heat-resistant bowls. Lay the toast on top of the soup and sprinkle it generously with the cheese. Place under a slow grill until the cheese melts and begins to brown. Serve immediately.

Tomato Soup

Hot or medium oven position or electric casserole
Approx. preparation time 8 minutes

The best tin of tomato soup never equals a good soup made with fresh tomatoes. Try this one when tomatoes are cheap. For 4 portions allow:

1 oz (25 g) fat streaky bacon,
  cut up
1 lb (400 g) onions finely sliced
  or shredded
1 lb (400 g) tomatoes, skinned
  and sliced
1 pt (500 ml) stock or water
  and a stock cube

2 cloves
salt and pepper to taste
½ tsp. (2·5 ml) sugar
a bouquet garni
2 tsp. (10 ml) tomato ketchup
2 tsp. (10 ml) sage

Heat the bacon in a stewpan over gentle heat until the fat begins to exude. Add the onions and continue to cook until these soften. Stir in the tomatoes and cook for a further minute or two. Remove from heat. Add the remaining ingredients. Either bring to the boil, cover closely and immediately slow cook or store and bring soup to the boil just before it goes in the oven or heated electric casserole.

When cooked, remove herbs and sieve, liquidize or beat well with a fork.

Fish

Fish cooked very slowly in the oven or an electric casserole is a delicious alternative to the quick methods of frying or grilling. These dishes (kedgeree excepted) will cook in 1 to 2 hours in an ultra-slow oven (hot or medium position) or electric casserole (*high*) but it can be left up to 5 hours in the oven (coolest) or casserole (*low*). The position or setting is therefore decided by the most convenient cooking time. The fish should be cooked as soon after purchase as possible.

A Flemish Fish Dish

See above for oven position or electric casserole setting
Approx. preparation time 5 minutes
For 2 portions allow:

¾–1 lb (300–400 g) cod or fresh haddock steaks or fillet

1 oz (25 g) butter or margarine

1 oz (25 g) onion, shredded

salt and pepper

nutmeg

4 fl. oz (100 ml) dry white wine or cider

2 tsp. (10 ml) lemon juice (fresh or bottled)

a bay leaf

a stick of celery (when available)

½ oz (12·5 g) breadcrumbs

1 tbs. (15 ml) chopped parsley

When using fillet, remove skin or get the fishmonger to do so.

Grease a shallow oven dish, slightly larger than the fish,

with some of the butter. Put in the fish, sprinkle with onion
and season with salt, pepper and nutmeg. Top with remaining butter, in small dabs. Pour the liquid round the fish and
lay the bay leaf and celery on top for flavour. For oven, slip
dish into a paper bag or wrap loosely in brown paper. For
electric casserole, see section on baking, page 24. Cook 1 to 5
hours.

Just before serving, remove bay leaf and celery. Strain
off liquor into a small saucepan. Boil it for about 5 minutes,
then add the breadcrumbs and parsley. Stir well and pour
over the fish.

Provençal Fish Pie

See page 31 for oven position or electric casserole setting
Approx. preparation time 7 minutes
For 2 portions allow :

12 oz–1 lb (300–400 g) cod, hake, haddock or coley fillet	2 tbs. (30 ml) chopped parsley
2½oz (62·5 g) butter	water and juice of ½ lemon, together ¼ pt (125 ml)
1 small onion, finely sliced	2 tsp. (10 ml) cornflour
4 tomatoes, skinned and chopped	salt and pepper
1 clove garlic, crushed in salt (optional)	8–10 fl. oz (200–250 ml) loosely packed fresh breadcrumbs

Melt ½ oz (12·5 g) of butter in a flame-proof dish or a frying pan and cook the onion and tomatoes over gentle heat
until soft but not brown. While these are cooking, remove
any skin and bones from the fish, and cut it into 1½″ (4 cm)
pieces. Add garlic and half the parsley to the onion and tomatoes. Put the cornflour in a cup and mix in the liquid. Add
this to the vegetables and stir until the sauce thickens, season
with salt and pepper. Mix in the fish. When using a frying
pan, transfer mixture to an oven dish. For oven, slip this into

a paper bag or wrap loosely in brown paper. For electric casserole, see section on baking, page 24. Cook 1 to 5 hours. Some time during the cooking melt the remaining 2 oz (50 g) of butter in a small pan and mix in the breadcrumbs and the rest of the parsley. A short while before serving, cover pie with buttered crumbs and brown under a grill.

Fillet of Cod or Haddock Special

See page 31 for oven position or electric casserole setting
Approx. preparation time 12 minutes
For 2 portions allow :

1 oz (25 g) butter	2½ fl. oz (62·5 ml) dry white
2 pieces of skinned fillet	wine or water and juice of ½
salt and pepper	lemon
1½ oz (37·5 g) onion, grated	1 tbs. (15 ml) cream
¼ lb (100 g) tomatoes, skinned	1 tbs. (15 ml) chopped parsley
and chopped	

Grease a shallow oven dish with half the butter. Put in the fish, and season with salt and pepper. Heat the rest of the butter in a small pan, and cook the onion over a gentle heat until clear. Add the tomato, and work it in with a wooden spoon. Stir the wine or water and lemon juice into the mixture and simmer for 5 minutes. Remove pan from heat. Stir in the cream, and pour the sauce over the fish. Cover the dish with greased paper. Cook 1 to 5 hours. For electric casserole, see section on baking, page 24. Garnish with the parsley just before serving. *Creamed Potatoes* (page 104) are good with this dish.

Scallops au Gratin

See page 31 for oven position or electric casserole setting
Approx. preparation time 10 minutes

For 2 portions allow:

2–5 scallops (according to size)	¼ tsp. (1·25 ml) salt
8–12 oz (200–300 g) fillet of cod, haddock or hake	pepper to taste
	¼ pt (125 ml) milk
1 oz (25 g) butter	2 oz (50 g) cheese, grated
1½ tbs. (22·5 ml) flour	brown breadcrumbs

Cut each scallop into about 6 pieces. Remove any skin or lurking bones from the fillet, and cut into cubes. Melt the butter in a flame-proof dish or a saucepan, and cook the scallops for a minute. Remove from heat, stir in the flour and seasoning, and gradually add the milk. Replace over heat and continue to stir until the sauce thickens. When using a saucepan, transfer the mixture to an oven dish. Add the fillet and half the cheese. Mix well. For oven, slip the dish into a paper bag or wrap loosely in brown paper. For electric casserole, see section on baking, page 24. Cook 1 to 5 hours.

When cooked, stir well to blend the fish juices into the sauce. Sprinkle the top with crumbs and the rest of the cheese. Brown under the grill and serve.

Shellfish and Sweet Corn Savoury

See page 124.

Soused Herrings or Mackerel

See page 31 for oven position or electric casserole setting
Approx. preparation time 2 minutes after fish are filleted.

These served cold with salad make a pleasant summer dish.
Ingredients:

filleted herrings or mackerel	a bay leaf (optional)
onion, shredded or finely sliced	vinegar and water in equal
salt	parts
a few peppercorns	

Roll up the fish, enclosing any roes. Fit them snugly into an oven dish. Add the onion, seasoning and bay leaf. Nearly cover with the vinegar and water. For oven, slip dish into a brown paper bag or make into a brown paper parcel. For electric casserole, see section on baking, page 24. Cook 1 to 5 hours.

Herrings or Mackerel Piquant

This good luncheon or supper dish is made with soused herrings or mackerel.
For 2 portions allow:

2 or 4 soused herrings or mackerel	½ tsp. (2·5 ml) made mustard
	¼ tsp. (1·25 ml) sugar
½ oz (12·5 g) butter or margarine	6 fl. oz (150 ml) liquor in which the fish was cooked
2 tsp. (10 ml) flour	

Lift the fish, either just cooked or cold, onto a clean dish. Heat fat in a small pan. Remove from heat and stir in the flour, mustard and sugar. When well blended, gradually stir in the liquid. Return pan to heat, and stir until the sauce thickens. Pour this over the fish. If the fish is still warm, the dish can now be served, otherwise heat it through in the oven for a short while.

Fish Cakes

These fish cakes are excellent and, when the sauce and cooked potato are to hand, far simpler to prepare than by the conventional method.
They are made with:

Fish cooked in Cream Sauce (page 37), *mashed potato, brown breadcrumbs.*

Mix the potato into the hot, newly cooked fish and sauce, allowing just enough potato to make a manageable but not very stiff mixture. Divide into portions, one for each fish cake. Put plenty of crumbs into a small pudding basin. Drop portions, one at a time, into the crumbs. Shake the basin so that the fish cakes bounce round and round, thus becoming circular and crumb-covered. Flatten the cakes slightly and put on a plate. Store until they are required, then fry. They should not be fried until they are cold and firm.

Kedgeree

(Cook as soon as prepared)
Coolest oven position; or electric casserole (*high*, 60–70 minutes).
Approx. preparation time 8 minutes
For 2 portions allow:

6 oz (150 g) *smoked haddock* *fillet*	1 *onion, finely chopped* *(optional)*
4 tsp. (20 ml) *vegetable oil*	½ pt (250 ml) *boiling water*
3 oz (75 g) *patna rice,* *unwashed*	

Skin fish. Cut into small pieces. Heat oil in a stewpan or flame-proof casserole. Fry rice and onion, stirring with a wooden spoon until the rice is a pale brown. Add the fish and boiling water. While still boiling, either cover with a well-fitting lid and place in the oven for up to 8 hours or transfer to a heated electric casserole.

Either serve while still hot with *knob of butter, chopped hard-boiled egg and chopped parsley* or cool before storing. To reheat, place chilled or frozen kedgeree with butter in a pan over gentle heat. Just before serving add hard-boiled egg and parsley.

FISH COOKED IN SAUCES

See page 31 for oven position or electric casserole setting
Approx. preparation time 2 minutes if sauce is ready.

All fish, from coley to turbot, is good cooked slowly in
sauce. The maximum flavour is retained as the fish juices
mingle with the sauce, and nothing could be simpler, especially when the chosen sauce is already to hand. Put a layer of
sauce on the bottom of an oven dish, place the fish on top
(first roll up flat fish fillets or skin coarse fish fillets), season
with salt and pepper. For the oven, slip the dish into a brown
paper bag or wrap loosely in brown paper. For the electric
casserole, see section on baking, page 24. Cook 1 to 5 hours.

When cooked, lift the fish carefully on to a warm dish.
Large fish (e.g. turbot and salmon) should first be skinned,
filleted and divided into portions. Stir the fish juices into the
sauce and pour over the fish. Serve hot, except in the case
of *Salmon Mayonnaise* and *Fish Salad*.

Fish in Cream Sauce

Use *a very thick white sauce*, to which a choice of the following has been added: *chopped parsley or fennel, salt and
pepper or a little anchovy sauce, a little tarragon vinegar,
sliced hard-boiled eggs, capers, shrimps or prawns*. See *Fish
Cakes* (page 35).

Fish in Tomato Sauce

Use *Tomato Sauce* (page 137).

Fish in Mustard Sauce

Use *Mustard Sauce* (page 147).

Salmon Mayonnaise and Fish Salad

Use *Canadian Mayonnaise* (page 149). Fish salad is improved when shrimps or prawns are mixed with the mayonnaise prior to cooking.

Fish in Sauce Tartare

Use *Canadian Mayonnaise* (page 149) to which *chopped parsley, finely chopped mixed pickles and a little tarragon vinegar* have been added. Herrings and mackerel are good cooked in this sauce.

Meat, Poultry and Game

CASSEROLED DISHES

Meat to be casseroled is cooked with other ingredients (one of which must be liquid or contain plenty of moisture) very slowly in a tightly covered container in the oven or in an electric casserole. It has been generally accepted that the food to be casseroled should first be brought very slowly to simmering point. But when using the Slow Cooking Method the food is not allowed to simmer and the result is certainly better. In some recipes the meat is first fried for a few seconds in hot fat and browned on all sides. This improves the flavour, but is inclined to toughen and slightly shrink the meat. Therefore only better cuts should be used for that method, as, once fried, however long and slowly the meat is subsequently cooked, it will never regain lost tenderness.

When root vegetables are included in ultra-slow meat casseroles, unless grated, they should first be either fried or boiled for about three minutes in a little water, which must be included in the liquid stipulated in the recipe.

Wine, used discreetly, often improves a dish. It is particularly good in casseroles, especially when they are slow cooked. This method minimizes the loss of alcoholic content and change of flavour that wine usually suffers when cooked.

Wine for cooking can be bought comparatively cheaply, and if you want to use it in these recipes, it can always be substituted for some other liquid. Cooking with wine differs from wine drinking in that there are no rules, except for certain special dishes, as to when red or white wine should be used. When experimenting, try using both in turn to find out which you prefer.

For reheating casseroled meat dishes see page 16.

Steak and Kidney

Most people have their own recipe for this classic dish, and, whether casseroled or steamed, they should all respond well to slow cooking. However, these two more unusual recipes for casseroled steak and kidney may provide a welcome change. Both are also satisfactory as a base for steak and kidney pudding or pie and can be made from stewing steak, shin, chuck steak, or skirt.

Casseroled Steak and Kidney (1)

Hot or medium oven position or electric casserole
Approx. preparation time 10 minutes
For 2 portions allow:

11 oz (275 g) beefsteak	2 oz (50 g) mushrooms, sliced
5 oz (125 g) ox kidney	a bay leaf
2½ tbs. (37·5 ml) flour	½ clove of garlic, crushed in
pinch of dry mustard	salt (optional)
¼ tsp. (1·25 ml) salt	¼ beef stock cube
a little ground pepper	a dash of Worcester sauce
a pinch of powdered mace	2 fl. oz (50 ml) port and
(optional)	8 fl. oz (200 ml) water or
1 medium onion, shredded	½ pt (250 ml) water

With a sharp knife remove excess fat from beef, cut it into thin slices, about 4″ x 3″ (10 cm x 7·5 cm). Cut the kidney into cubes, equal in number to the beef slices. Place flour and dry seasoning in a paper bag, and shake in it the meat, onion and mushrooms. When these are well coated, tip the lot on to a plate. Wrap a piece of beef round each piece of kidney and include a slice of mushroom. Place these rolls, the rest of the mushrooms, the onion, the bay leaf and garlic in a casserole (oven or electric). Add crumbled stock cube, sauce and liquid. Cover closely and cook by day or night.

When this dish is wanted for *Steak and Kidney Pudding* or *Steak and Kidney Pie*, see pages 79 and 80.

Casseroled Steak and Kidney (2)

(A two-stage recipe)

Stage 1. Hot or medium oven position or electric casserole
Approx. preparation time 2 minutes
For 2 portions allow :

½ lb (200 g) beefsteak
(the meat in one piece)
¼ lb (100 g) ox kidney (also
uncut)

8 fl. oz (200 ml) stock or water
and ¾ crumbled beef stock
cube
salt and pepper
bouquet garni or a bay leaf
(optional)

Place the beef and kidney in an oven casserole (with only a little space around the meat) or in an electric casserole. Add all the other ingredients. Cover securely, and cook by day or night, as convenient, until the meat is really tender.

When cooked, remove herbs and cool meat rapidly in its liquor. Stage 2 can be carried out as soon as the fat has congealed, or within a day or so if kept in a refrigerator, or after a much longer time if stored in a freezer.

Stage 2. Approx. preparation time 10 minutes

In addition to the *ingredients cooked in Stage 1,* allow:

*a rasher of bacon, cut into
    pieces*
1 or 2 onions, finely sliced
*½ clove garlic crushed in
    salt (optional)*

*a little flour, seasoning and
    flavouring to taste*
tomato purée (optional)

Put a good tablespoon (15 ml) of the fat from the top of the casserole in a saucepan or flame-proof serving dish over gentle heat. If there is not enough, make up the quantity with dripping. Add bacon, onion and garlic. Cover and cook gently for a few minutes. Meanwhile remove steak and kidney from its jellified liquor, and cut into neat pieces. When the onion is clear, remove pan from heat, and add just enough flour to absorb the fat. If a tomato flavour is wanted, now add a little tomato purée. Stir with a wooden spoon, and, when the flour and fat are well blended, gradually add the liquor from Stage 1. Replace pan over heat, and continue stirring until the sauce thickens. Taste, and determine the flavour. Add more seasoning if needed, and any of the following, as fancied: a little sauce – Worcester or one of the many other sauces on the market – a small glass of sherry, a little black treacle or Barbados sugar. Add the meat and either simmer gently for about 2 minutes and serve, or cool, store and re-heat when required.

When this dish is wanted for a *Steak and Kidney Pudding* or *Pie,* see pages 79 and 80.

Stiphado (Greek Beef Stew)

Hot oven position or electric casserole
Approx. preparation time 10 minutes

For 2 portions allow:

8–10 oz (200–250 g) chuck steak	½ clove garlic, crushed in salt (optional)
salt and pepper	2 tbs. (30 ml) or a 2¼ oz
1½ tbs. (22·5 ml) olive oil	(56·25 g) tomato purée
½ lb (200 g) onions, sliced	3½ fl. oz (87·5 ml) red wine

Cut the beef into pieces about 2" x 3" (5 cm x 7·5 cm). Rub these well with salt and pepper. Heat oil in a large frying pan, and fry the meat, onions and garlic until the onions begin to brown. Transfer mixture to a casserole (oven or electric). Stir in the tomato purée and wine. Cover and cook by day or night.

Goulash

Hot or medium oven position or electric casserole
Approx. preparation time 15 minutes
For 2 portions allow:

½ lb (200 g) lean stewing beef or veal	1 tsp. (5 ml) tomato purée
1 oz (25 g) dripping or lard	1 large prune, stoned and cut up (optional)
½ lb (200 g) onions, sliced	2–3 tbs. (30–45 ml) stock or water and a small piece of stock cube
½ clove garlic, crushed in salt	
2 tsp. (10 ml) paprika	½–¾ lb (200–300 g) boiled or pressure-cooked potatoes
½ tsp. (2·5 ml) flour	
⅛ tsp. (0·62 ml) salt	1–1½ tbs. (15–22·5 ml) yoghourt (optional)
a little black pepper	
¾ tsp. (3·75 ml) caraway seeds	
a pinch of dried marjoram	

Remove fat, gristle and skin from meat, and cut it into fairly large cubes. Melt fat in a flame-proof casserole, a stew-pan or a frying pan, and fry the onions and garlic until the onion begins to soften. Add the meat, stir with a wooden spoon, and when it begins to brown, sprinkle in the paprika and flour. Continue to stir for about two minutes, then remove from heat. When using a frying pan, transfer mixture to a casserole (oven or electric). Add seasoning, caraway seeds, marjoram, tomato purée, prunes and liquid. Mix well, cover closely and cook by day or night.

When cooked, either add the hot cooked potatoes and yoghourt and serve, or store and add cold potatoes prior to slow reheating, mixing in the yoghourt just before serving.

Flemish Carbonnades (or Carbonados) of Beef

(Cook well in advance of serving)
Hot or medium oven position or electric casserole
Approx. preparation time 15 minutes

This dish, cooked with ale, has its own deliciously distinctive flavour. The meat should melt in the mouth – slow cooking ensures this, and longer than eight hours may be necessary. In that case the heat can be raised slightly for the extra cooking provided the meat is not allowed to boil. Neck, top shoulder and thin flank of beef are all suitable cuts.
For 2–3 portions allow:

1 lb (400 g) beef	¾ tbs. (12 ml) flour
salt and pepper	8 fl. oz (200 ml) brown ale
1½ oz (37.5 g) lard or dripping	1 clove garlic, crushed in salt
1½ oz (37.5 g) lean diced gammon	1 tsp. (5 ml) dark, moist sugar
	a bouquet garni (optional)
7 oz (175 g) onion, shredded	1 tsp. (5 ml) vinegar
½ oz (12.5 g) butter	

Cut the meat into pieces about 2″ (5 cm) long and 1″ (2.5 cm) thick, and season well with salt and pepper. Heat lard in a frying pan and brown the beef, adding the gammon halfway through the process. Lift the meat and gammon onto a plate. Put the onion into the pan and fry until it begins to brown, then lift onto a second plate. Pour away any surplus fat, and heat the butter. Stir in the flour with a wooden spoon, and when well blended, gradually add the ale, stirring continuously until the sauce thickens. Add garlic and sugar. Pour the sauce into a casserole (oven or electric) and add alternate layers of onion, meat and gammon, also the bouquet garni. Press down the solids until they are covered by sauce. Fasten lid firmly, and cook by day or at night.

When cooked, cool rapidly so that any congealed fat may be removed from the top. Before the dish is reheated for serving, add 1 tsp. (5 ml) vinegar.

Beef Olives

(Cook well in advance of serving)
Hot or medium oven position or electric casserole
Approx. preparation time 25 minutes

An excellent, inexpensive party dish. Ask the butcher to slice the meat for you – his knife can cut it much thinner.
For 4 portions allow:

¾ lb (300 g) thinly cut buttock
  steak
9 tbs. (135 ml) fresh breadcrumbs
3 tbs. (45 ml) shredded suet
the grated rind and juice of a
  small lemon
1 tbs. (15 ml) chopped parsley
1 tsp. (5 ml) dried mixed herbs
seasoning

1 egg
1 tbs. (15 ml) flour
¼ tsp. (1·25 ml) salt and a
  little pepper
1 oz (25 g) butter or dripping
1 small onion, finely chopped
½ pt (250 ml) stock or water
¼ lb (100 g) mushrooms, sliced,
  or a green pepper, seeded
  and sliced

Cut the beef slices into pieces about 4″ x 2″ (10 cm x 5 cm). Beat each piece until it is flat. A cutlet bat, wooden rolling pin, the edge of a saucer, or the bottom of a milk bottle can

be used for this. Place the crumbs, suet, lemon, herbs and
seasoning in a mixing bowl. Mix well. Beat the egg in a cup,
and add sufficient to the ingredients in the basin to bind
them into a manageable stuffing. Spread some of this onto
each piece of beef. Roll them up and fasten with thick white
cotton or very fine string. Shake each olive in a paper bag
containing the flour, salt and pepper. Heat the fat in a flame-
proof casserole or frying pan. Brown the olives and set them
aside. Now fry the onion, and, when soft, shake the remaining seasoned flour from the bag into the fat, gradually add
the liquid, and stir with a wooden spoon until it thickens.
Remove from heat and allow to cool. Stir the remaining egg
into the sauce. Add the olives, or, when using a frying pan,
arrange them in a casserole (oven or electric) and pour the
sauce over them. Surround the meat with the mushrooms or
pepper. Cover and cook by day or night.

When cooked, cool dish rapidly so that the unwanted
congealed fat can be removed from the top. Reheat the
olives shortly before the meal – they are very good served
with *Creamed Potatoes* (page 104).

Beef Stewed in Beer

Medium or cool oven position or electric casserole
Approx. preparation time 5 minutes
A German recipe.
For 4–6 portions allow :

2 lb (800 g) rump steak	2½ fl. oz (62·5 ml) vinegar
4–6 rindless bacon rashers, sliced No. 4	1 tbs. (15 ml) black treacle
2 or 3 onions, shredded	2 cloves
beer and water in equal quantities	1 bay leaf
	salt and pepper

Beat beef well to flatten, roll it up, tie with string, and place on top of the bacon and onion in a casserole (oven or electric). Just cover the meat with the beer and water mixture. Add remaining ingredients. Cover, and cook by day or night.

Beef Creole

Medium or cool oven position or electric casserole
Approx. preparation time 8 minutes

Delicious, and simple to prepare. In the Latin-American recipe, rump of beef is used, but other more economical cuts, such as topside or chuck, are equally satisfactory.
For 4–6 portions allow:

4 slices rindless streaky bacon	a little pepper
a 2 lb (800 g) joint of beef	1 lb (400 g) tomatoes, skinned
1 green pepper, seeded and	and chopped, or a 14 oz
finely sliced (optional, but an	(350 g) tin peeled tomatoes
asset)	1 lb (400 g) onions, finely
¼ tsp. (1·25 ml) salt	chopped

Use a casserole (oven or electric) a little larger than the beef. Lay the bacon on the bottom, with the meat on top. Add the seasoning and arrange all the vegetables on and around the meat. Cover, and cook by day or night.

This is a good dish to cook by day for the evening meal. When cooked overnight, or not wanted immediately, it can, if it has been rapidly cooled and stored in a refrigerator, be reheated before serving in one of the following ways: (1) return casserole to oven (gas mark 3, 170° C., 325° F.) and warm through without boiling; (2) transfer the dish from the casserole to a pressure cooker. Cook for ½ minute at 15 lbs pressure; (3) remove the beef and pour the sauce into a wide, shallow stewpan or flame-proof casserole. Heat, but do not boil. Carve meat, and just before serving, put the slices in the hot sauce, leaving them long enough to ensure they are heated through.

Beef Catalan

Medium or cool oven position or electric casserole
Approx. preparation time 10 minutes

This Spanish way of cooking beef can be adapted to a more economical, but still good, English version.

For 6–8 portions allow :

2 lb (800 g) topside
6 oz (150 g) bacon rashers,
  sliced No. 4
½ lb (200 g) onions, finely
  sliced
2 carrots, sliced
2 oz (50 g) mushrooms, sliced
  (optional)
1 clove garlic, crushed in salt
a few peppercorns
a pinch of nutmeg

a bouquet garni
½ oz (12·5 g) butter
¾ lb (300 g) tomatoes, chopped
  and skinned, or a 14 oz
  (350 g) tin of tomatoes
1 tsp. (5 ml) black treacle
2 fl. oz (50 ml) red wine and
  1 tsp. (15 ml) brandy, or, for
  the English version, 6 fl. oz
  (150 ml) draft or bottled still,
  dry cider

Place the meat resting on the bacon and surrounded by all the other ingredients except the tomatoes, treacle and liquids, in a flame-proof casserole or a stewpan. Cover. Place over a low heat and simmer very gently until the vegetables begin to brown. Add remaining ingredients and simmer again for a few minutes. If applicable, transfer to electric casserole at this point. Add enough water just to cover meat. Fasten lid and cook by day or night.

This dish can be reheated by one of the methods given for *Beef Creole* (page 47).

Oxtail

(A two-stage recipe)
Stage 1. Hottest oven position or electric casserole
Approx. preparation time 2 minutes
For 3–4 portions allow:

1 *oxtail, cut up*	*salt and pepper*
16 *fl. oz* (400 *ml*) *water*	*bouquet garni (optional)*

Prepare and cook the oxtail as given for *Casseroled Steak and Kidney* (2), Stage 1, page 41. The cooked meat should come away from the bones with ease. If not, slow cook for longer or cook for a short spell at a higher temperature.

Stage 2. Approx. preparation time 10 minutes

In addition to the cooked ingredients from Stage 1, allow:

1 *large onion, sliced*	*seasoning to taste*
½ *clove garlic, crushed in salt*	3 *oz* (75 *g*) *macaroni*
(*optional*)	1–2 *oz* (25–50 *g*) *grated cheese*
flour	

Heat 2 tbs. (30 ml) of the fat from the top of the oxtail in a flame-proof casserole or saucepan, over gentle heat. Add onion and garlic, cover, and cook until the onion is soft. Remove from heat and stir in enough flour to absorb the fat. Gradually add the oxtail liquor, probably in jelly form. Stir over heat until the sauce thickens. Add the oxtail and seasoning, and heat well. Cook the macaroni. Mix the cheese with the macaroni and serve either in its own dish or as a border round the oxtail.

Casseroled Liver

Medium or cool oven position or electric casserole
Approx. preparation time 12 minutes

Any kind of liver can be used for this dish, though with

this method it seems more sensible to use the cheaper ox or pig liver. These are inclined to be strong and tough when fried or grilled, whereas the more expensive calf and sheep liver are delicious after a few minutes in the frying pan or under the grill.

For 2 portions allow:

½ lb (200 g) liver
1 tbs. (15 ml) flour
¼ tsp. (1·25 ml) salt
a little ground pepper
¼ tsp. (1·25 ml) dry mustard
1 tbs. (15 ml) butter, oil or
  dripping
2 bacon rashers, cut into pieces
1 large onion, sliced

1 tomato, skinned and sliced
½ clove garlic, crushed in salt
  (optional)
¼ pt (125 ml) stock or water
  and ¼ beef stock cube
sprigs of parsley, thyme and
  marjoram or ¼ tsp. (1·25 ml)
  mixed herbs

Wash liver well in warm water, removing any tubes, fat and skin, and cut into ¼″ (½ cm) slices. Shake these in a paper bag with the flour and seasonings. Heat the fat in a flame-proof casserole, stewpan or frying pan. Fry the liver and bacon until the liver begins to brown, then lift onto a plate. Tip the onion, tomato and garlic into the fat, and sprinkle in the rest of the seasoned flour from the bag. Blend this together with the liquid into the vegetables and stir for about 3 minutes. Remove from heat. When using a frying pan, transfer mixture to a casserole (oven or electric). Add the liver, bacon and herbs. Cover, and cook by day or night.

Casseroled Kidney

(A two-stage recipe)

When kidneys are cooked very slowly the gravy tastes as much of kidney as the kidneys themselves – this makes a little go a long way. As sheep's kidneys are so good grilled or cooked quickly in butter, this recipe is particularly valuable for the cheaper, more strongly flavoured kidneys.

Stage 1. Hot or medium oven position or electric casserole
Approx. preparation time 5 minutes
For 2 portions allow:

6–8 oz (150–200 g) ox or calf kidney, or 3 pig kidneys, or 4–5 sheep kidneys
1 bacon rasher, cut up
a few slices of green pepper, cut up (optional)
2 oz (50 g) mushrooms, sliced (optional)

¼ pt (125 ml) stock or water or cheap red wine or 2½ fl. oz (62·5 ml) each sherry and water
salt
pepper

Cut up kidneys and place them on the bottom of a small oven casserole or an electric casserole. Add all the other ingredients. Cover and cook by day or night.

Once cooked, cool kidneys rapidly. Then either carry out Stage 2 and serve, or store and complete the dish when required.

Stage 2. Approx. preparation time 10 minutes
In addition to the ingredients from Stage 1, allow:

1 or 2 onions, finely sliced
½ clove garlic, crushed in salt (optional)
a little flour
seasoning

Tabasco or soy sauce (optional)
2 pieces of toast, or boiled or fried rice
1 tbs. (15 ml) chopped parsley, or a few sprigs of watercress

Put 1 tbs. (15 ml) of the fat from the top of the kidneys in a saucepan or flame-proof casserole over a gentle heat; if there is not enough fat, make up with butter or dripping. Cook the onion and garlic in the covered pan until soft but not brown. Remove from heat, and stir in sufficient flour to absorb the fat. Remove kidneys from casserole, and set aside.

Stir the rest into the fat and onion mixture. Replace pan over heat and stir until the sauce thickens. Taste, add seasoning as required, and, if liked, a little soy or Tabasco sauce. Add the kidney, reduce heat and warm through. As this is a rich dish, rice may be preferable to toast. Either boil rice during Stage 2, or cook *Fried Rice*, page 126, in the slow oven with the kidneys and reheat while Stage 2 is carried out. Serve the kidneys either on top of hot toast or surrounded by rice. Garnish with parsley or watercress.

Veal Casserole

Hot or medium oven position or electric casserole
Approx. preparation time 12 minutes
For 2 portions allow :

12 oz (300 g) stewing veal	2 tsp. (10 ml) flour
1 oz (25 g) butter	¼ tsp. (1·25 ml) salt
1 onion, sliced	a little pepper
1 tomato, skinned and sliced	2½ fl. oz (62·5 ml) each white
either 2 oz (50 g) mushrooms,	wine and water or ¼ pt
sliced, or 1 green pepper,	(125 ml) stock or water and
seeded and sliced	¼ stock cube

Remove fat and skin from meat and cut into fairly small pieces. Heat butter in a flame-proof casserole or a stewpan or frying pan. Cook meat until just brown, and set aside. Fry the onion until soft. Add flour and seasoning, and stir with a wooden spoon until the flour browns. Remove from heat and stir in the liquids. When blended, add the meat and remaining vegetables. If using a frying pan, transfer mixture to a casserole (oven or electric). Cover and cook during the day or night.

Irish Stew

Medium oven position or electric casserole
Approx. preparation time 15 minutes

This is an Irish stew that anyone from that country will acknowledge as the real thing. It is easy on the budget, and just right for a cold day. Ask the butcher to cut up the meat for you.

For 2 good portions allow :

boiling water	*salt*
1 lb (400 g) *potatoes*	*pepper*
¼ lb (100 g) *onions*	1 *tbs.* (15 ml) *chopped parsley*
½–¾ lb (200–300 g) *middle*	*(optional)*
neck of lamb	

Peel and cut potatoes into ½″ (1 cm) slices. Put these in a saucepan and cover with boiling water. Let them boil for 5 to 8 minutes, then strain. Meanwhile peel and thinly slice the onions, put them in a small pan, add 3 fl. oz (75 ml) boiling water and cook them for two minutes. Lay the meat, cut in portions, on the bottom of a flame-proof casserole or stew-pan with a closely fitting lid which has room for all the ingredients. Sprinkle generously with salt and pepper. On the meat place a layer of onions with their liquor, and more salt and pepper. Top with the potatoes, sprinkled with salt and pepper. If the dish is to be cooked immediately cover the pan and place it over gentle heat for a minute or two before cooking in an oven or heated electric casserole. The uncooked dish can be stored in a refrigerator for up to 14 hours by placing a damp cloth on top of the potatoes beneath the lid. After storing, remove cloth, and place pan over a very gentle heat for 5 minutes before slow cooking.

To serve : mash the potato and onion with the gravy. Arrange on a hot dish with the meat on top. Garnish with parsley.

Economy Stew

Hot or medium oven position or electric casserole
Approx. preparation time 15 minutes
Cook as soon as prepared

Though this dish contains only a little meat, it has a good meaty flavour.

For 3 portions allow:

½ lb (200 g) scrag of lamb, cut into neat pieces	1 parsnip, diced
2 tsp. (10 ml) flour	1 turnip, diced, or ½ lb (200 g) swede, diced
¼ tsp. (1·25 ml) salt and a little pepper	1 large carrot, sliced
1 oz (25 g) dripping	1 tbs. (15 ml) pearl barley
1 large onion, thinly sliced	a bouquet garni
	½ pt (250 ml) boiling water

Shake the meat in a paper bag with flour and seasoning. Heat the fat in a flame-proof casserole or a frying pan, and fry the meat until it browns, then set aside. Put the vegetables in the hot fat, shake remaining seasoned flour over them, and fry until they are brown, stirring gently with a wooden spoon. Remove pan from heat and add the meat. When using a frying pan, transfer ingredients to a casserole (oven or electric). Add the barley and bouquet garni, and pour the boiling water round the sides of the casserole. Cover tightly. If the lid does not fit properly put a piece of foil over the dish, under the lid. Cook immediately.

When cooked, take out the herbs, cut up the meat, removing bones and sinew. Mix meat thoroughly with the vegetables.

Lamb and Tomato Sauce

Hot or medium oven position or electric casserole
Approx. preparation time 10 minutes

For 2 portions allow :

¼ oz (6·25 g) butter or margarine	¼ tsp. (1·25 ml) salt
just over 1 lb (400 g) best end or middle neck	a little pepper or a dash of Tabasco
1 small onion, finely sliced	1 tsp. (5 ml) sugar
¼ lb (100 g) tomatoes, skinned and chopped	1 fl. oz (25 ml) vinegar
	3 fl. oz (75 ml) stock or water
	1 tsp. (5 ml) sago

Heat fat gently in a flame-proof casserole or a frying pan. Brown the meat, and set aside. Fry the onion until soft. Add the tomato, work it into the fat and onion with a wooden spoon and cook for a minute. Stir in the rest of the ingredients. When using a frying pan, transfer mixture to a casserole (oven or electric). Put in the meat, cover and cook by day or night.

When cooked, and served immediately, skim off fat and cut meat into neat pieces. When the dish has been stored the cold congealed fat should be removed and the meat cut up before reheating.

Bredee

Medium or cool oven position or electric casserole
Approx. preparation time 8 minutes
A tasty South African dish.
For 2 portions allow :

1 lb (400 g) lean middle neck lamb	a 14 oz (350 g) tin tomatoes
½ oz (12·5 g) butter or dripping	¼ tsp. (1·25 ml) chilli sauce
	½ tsp. (2·5 ml) salt
1 medium onion, sliced	¼ tsp. (1·25 ml) pepper
	1 tsp. (5 ml) sugar

Cut the meat into small pieces. Heat fat in a flame-proof casserole or a frying pan and fry the onion until it begins to brown. Add the meat and fry quickly, stirring continually. When the meat is brown on all sides, add the other ingredients and, still stirring, cook for a further 2 minutes. If using a frying pan, transfer mixture to a casserole (oven or electric). Cover and cook as convenient.

When cooked, either spoon off top fat and serve, or store and reheat as required, having first removed congealed top fat.

Serve with *Fried Rice* (page 126) or macaroni.

Curried Chops

Medium or cool oven position or electric casserole
Approx. preparation time 10 minutes
This dish must be prepared well in advance of cooking so that the chops can marinate for at least 12 hours.
For 2 portions allow :

¼ oz (6·25 g) butter, dripping or olive oil	1 tsp. (5 ml) curry powder
2 lamb chops	¼ tsp. (1·25 ml) salt
1 small onion, finely sliced	a little pepper
½ a small cooking apple, cut up	½ tsp. (2·5 ml) Worcester sauce
1 tbs. (15 ml) currants or sultanas	1½ fl. oz (37·5 ml) each of vinegar and water

Heat the fat in a small frying pan and brown the chops. Transfer these to a small casserole. Now fry the onion in the same fat until brown. Remove from heat. Add the apple and currants. Stir in the curry powder, seasoning, sauce and finally the vinegar and water. Pour this mixture over the chops. Allow the dish to get cold. Cover and store it in a refrigerator for at least 12 hours, turning the chops now and then. Cook in oven or transfer to heated electric casserole.

Serve very hot with *Fried Rice* (page 126) or *Creamed Potatoes* (page 104).

Stuffed Lambs' Hearts
(A two-stage recipe)

Hearts cooked this way are deliciously tender, and make a nourishing, inexpensive meal.

Stage 1. Hot or medium oven position or electric casserole

Approx. preparation time 10 minutes

For 2 portions allow :

2 lambs' hearts	a pinch each of nutmeg, salt
1½ tbs. (22·5 ml) grated stale bread	and pepper
	a little beaten egg or stock
½ oz (12·5 g) shredded suet or melted butter or margarine	about 3 fl. oz (75 ml) dry cider or beer with the same in
1 tsp. (5 ml) chopped parsley	water, or 6 fl. oz (150 ml)
½ tsp. (2·5 ml) powdered thyme	stock or water
1 tsp. (5 ml) grated lemon rind	

Wash hearts thoroughly and remove any tubes. Place all dry ingredients in a basin, mix well and bind them with egg or stock. Stuff the hearts and stand them upright in a casserole with a closely fitting lid, or an electric casserole – poaching rings or pastry cutters are useful for holding them in position. Pour in the liquid; it should come halfway up the hearts. Cover and cook by day or night, until the hearts are really tender.

When cooked, cool hearts rapidly in their liquor, after removing any props. Stage 2 can be carried out as soon as the hearts are cold. They can be stored for a day or two before the dish is completed if kept in a refrigerator.

Stage 2. As given for *Casseroled Steak and Kidney* (2), Stage 2 (page 42).

The bacon is optional.

Devilled Pork Chops

Medium or cool oven position or electric casserole
Approx. preparation time 5 minutes

A dish for those who enjoy the hot chili flavour. It should
be prepared well in advance of cooking so that the chops can
marinate for at least 12 hours.

For 2 portions allow:

a little butter	2 tsp. (10 ml) grated onion
2 pork chops 1"–2" (2·5–5 cm) thick	⅛ tsp. (0·62 ml) dry mustard
	1 tsp. (5 ml) Worcester sauce
2 tsp. (10 ml) chili sauce or to taste	¼ tsp. (1·25 ml) salt
	2 fl. oz (50 ml) water
1 tbs. (15 ml) lemon juice, fresh or bottled	2 tsp. (10 ml) black treacle or moist brown sugar (optional)

Well grease a flame-proof casserole or a frying pan with
butter, and sear the chops. When using a frying pan, transfer the chops to a casserole. Mix all the other ingredients in
a basin and pour the mixture over the chops. When cool,
cover and store for at least 12 hours before slow cooking.

Serve with a green vegetable or watercress and a choice
of Fried Rice (page 126), Creamed Potatoes (page 104), or
Butter or Haricot Beans (pages 104 to 105). These can be
cooked at the same time as the chops.

Gammon Rashers Cooked in Sauce
See page 89.

Pickled Pork and Beans

Cook and cool Pickled Pork as given on page 73, and, in the
same oven load, cook some Butter Beans (pages 104 to 105).
Use fat from the top of the pork, with a little flour, a little

pork liquor (if not too fatty), milk and chopped parsley to make a sauce for the beans.

Chicken and Rice

Medium or cool oven position or electric casserole
Approx. preparation time 15 minutes (cook as soon as prepared)
For 4–5 portions allow:

1 oz (25 g) butter or margarine	3½ oz (87.5 g) patna rice, unwashed
about 2 lb (800 g) chicken joints	12 fl. oz (300 ml) boiling liquid made with liquid from
¼ lb (100 g) bacon, cut up	tomatoes, water and ½
tomatoes, strained from small tin	chicken stock cube
1 tbs. (15 ml) vegetable oil	seasoning to taste
3 medium onions, chopped	

Heat fat in a pan. Fry chicken and bacon until chicken is brown. Add cut up tomatoes. Cook a further 2 minutes. Set aside. Heat oil in a flame-proof casserole or a stewpan over medium heat. Add onion and rice. Stir and cook until onion is transparent and rice a pale brown. Add bacon, tomato and fat from pan, the boiling liquid and seasoning. Stir well. When mixture reboils, add chicken. Immediately either cover tightly and place in oven or transfer to a heated electric casserole.

Chicken Marengo

Medium or cool oven position or electric casserole
Approx. preparation time 15 minutes

A good party dish, adapted from one said to have been served to Napoleon after the battle of Marengo.

For 2 portions allow:

½ oz (12·5 g) butter
4 pickling onions or 1 medium
   onion, sliced
¼ lb (100 g) mushrooms, sliced
2 chicken joints
1 tsp. (5 ml) flour
1 tbs. (15 ml) olive oil
1 tomato, skinned and sliced
1 tsp. (5 ml) tomato purée
salt and pepper to taste

⅛ chicken stock cube
2 tbs (30 ml) dry white wine or
   dry cider
2 tbs. (30 ml) water
½ clove garlic, crushed in salt
   (optional)
Garnish: Chopped parsley,
   croutons of fried bread
   (optional)

Melt the butter in a small saucepan and cook the onion and mushrooms until they begin to brown, then set aside. While these are cooking, sprinkle flour over the chicken, heat the oil gently in a flame-proof casserole, a shallow stew-pan or a frying pan, and brown the chicken all over. Take out the chicken, and sautez the tomato and tomato purée, stirring them into the oil with a wooden spoon. Remove from heat, and when using a frying pan or stewpan, tip the contents into a casserole (oven or electric). Season to taste with salt and pepper and add the crumbled stock cube, the liquids, the chicken, the browned onion and mushrooms and garlic. Cover closely and cook by day or night.

Serve garnished with parsley and, if liked, small triangles of bread fried in butter or lard.

Curry of Chicken or Other Meats

Hot oven position for boiling fowl; or electric casserole
Medium or cool oven position for roasting or frying chicken
Approx. preparation time 15 minutes

Rabbit or any casserole meat can be used for this recipe, as an alternative to chicken, in appropriate oven position or in electric casserole.

For 2 portions allow:

1 oz (25 g) butter or margarine
1 onion, finely sliced
1 clove garlic, crushed in salt
  (optional)
1 small cooking apple
1½ tbs. (22·5 ml) flour
2 tsp. (10 ml) curry powder
½ tsp. (2·5 ml) salt

a shake of Tabasco (optional)
1 tsp. (5 ml) black treacle
6 fl. oz (150 ml) milk
6 fl. oz (150 ml) hot water
1 tsp. (5 ml) lemon juice, fresh
  or bottled
2 joints of chicken or rabbit or
  ½ lb (200 g) casserole meat

Heat the fat in a flame-proof casserole or a medium sized stewpan over moderate heat. Add the onion and garlic, and cover utensil. Peel, core and chop up the apple and add to the onion. Stir with a wooden spoon, lower heat, cover again and cook until the apple is mushy. Remove from heat, sprinkle in the dry ingredients and stir until well blended. Add the treacle and Tabasco. Gradually mix in the milk and water. Return to heat and stir until the sauce thickens. Remove from heat, stir in lemon juice and test flavour, adding more salt and treacle if needed. Allow to cool. Add chicken. Cover. Cook as convenient. If applicable, first transfer mixture to an electric casserole.

Of course rice, boiled or fried, must be served with curry. *Fried Rice* (page 126) can be cooked in the oven at the same time. But rice alone does not complete a curry: it is those delicious little odds and ends – salty, sweet and piquant, known as sambals – that add the finishing touch. These should be assembled shortly before serving and arranged in little dishes or saucers. Choose a selection from these suggested sambals.

salted nuts
chopped anchovies
chopped stuffed olives
potato crisps

chopped peppers
Bombay duck (dried fish that
  can be bought in tins. Must
  be fried)

chopped cucumber
chopped tomato
peeled grapes
lychees
diced apple with lemon juice
diced beetroot
chopped preserved or
   crystallized ginger
dried fruit

sliced banana
pineapple pieces
mango chutney
sliced gherkins
cocktail onions
chopped pickled walnuts
chopped mixed pickles
chopped pickled pears (page
   144)

Red-cooked Chicken

(Cook as soon as prepared)
Medium or cool oven position or electric casserole
Approx. preparation time 6 minutes

This Chinese recipe is a good way of giving flavour to broiler chicken joints.

For 2 portions allow:

a very little fat for frying	*1 fl. oz (25 ml) soy sauce*
2 chicken joints	*1 tsp. (5 ml) sugar*
1 small onion, sliced	*2 tsp. (10 ml) sherry*
6 fl. oz (150 ml) water	*salt to taste*

Heat fat in a frying pan and fry chicken and onion. Remove chicken when well browned, and place in a casserole (oven or electric). Add the remaining ingredients to the onion in the pan and, when boiling, pour over the chicken. Cover and cook immediately.

Serve with boiled rice, or *Fried Rice* (page 126) cooked at the same time as the chicken.

Coq au Vin

Medium oven position or electric casserole
Approx. preparation time 15 minutes

This classic French dish lends itself well to slow cooking. The chicken must be jointed, but don't use chicken joints. Try to get a plump free-range bird and ask the butcher to cut it up for you.

For 4–6 portions allow:

1 oz (25 g) butter	a small glass brandy
1 tsp. (5 ml) olive oil	¼ lb (100 g) button mushrooms
10 shallots, halved, or 2 to 3 onions, thickly sliced	a clove of garlic, crushed in salt (optional)
a chicken, approx. 4 lb (2 kg)	1 tsp. (5 ml) sugar
a ¼" (½ cm) slice lean bacon, cut into cubes	salt and pepper
	8 fl. oz (200 ml) red wine

Heat the fats gently in a deep flame-proof casserole, a self-basting roaster, or a stewpan with a tightly fitting lid. Put in the shallots or onions, cover and cook till soft. Remove these from container and set aside. Raise heat and brown the chicken joints and bacon uncovered. Warm the brandy, pour it over the chicken and set alight. Remove from heat. Add the onions and other ingredients. Cover, and cook as convenient in the oven or an electric casserole.

When cooked, the sauce can be thickened with a little cornflour mixed with cream or top of milk. Serve with *Rice Balls* (page 127) cooked in the oven with the chicken, or small squares of bread fried in butter.

Pigeons

When available, these are never expensive, and, cooked slowly, are always deliciously tender. Many people find a plump pigeon provides an ample meal for two, though good healthy appetites may welcome a bird apiece.

Pigeons with Mushrooms or Peppers Cooked in Sherry

Hot or medium oven position or electric casserole
Approx. preparation time 7 minutes
For 2 pigeons allow :

olive oil	¼ lb (100 g) mushrooms,
a little flour	cleaned and sliced, or 1
salt and pepper	medium pepper, seeded and
4 thin rashers streaky bacon	sliced
1 onion, grated	2½ fl. oz (62·5 ml) sherry
1 stick celery, cut up (optional)	2½ fl. oz (62·5 ml) water
1 medium carrot, sliced	½ oz (12·5 g) butter

Brush the pigeons lavishly with oil, dredge with flour and season well with salt and pepper. Cover the breasts with bacon, and place birds with the vegetables in a casserole with a tightly fitting lid or an electric casserole. Add the liquid and butter, in small dabs. Cover and cook by day or night.

Pigeon and Green Pea Casserole

Hot or medium oven position
Approx. preparation time 6 minutes
For 2 pigeons allow :

olive oil	2 tsp. (10 ml) lemon juice,
salt and pepper	fresh or bottled
a pinch of powdered ginger	a sprig of parsley
(optional)	a pinch of dried thyme
4 thin slices streaky bacon	a small packet of frozen peas
1 onion, shredded	¼ pt (125 ml) water or stock
½ tsp. (2·5 ml) sugar	(less when the peas are still
	icy)

Brush the pigeons thickly with oil, sprinkle with salt, pepper and ginger, and cover breasts with bacon. Place birds in an oven casserole with a tightly fitting lid with all the other ingredients except the peas and water. These must not be added until just before the pigeons are cooked. This can be done at night or during the day.

Jugged Hare (1)

Medium or cool oven position or electric casserole

This is a grand party dish. The initial preparation must be done well in advance. The preparation before cooking will take approximately 10 minutes.

Ask the butcher to dissect the hare, and make sure he gives you the blood.

For 6–8 portions allow:

1 *hare*	*about 1 tbs. (15 ml) flour*
½ *bottle red wine*	1 *clove garlic, crushed in salt*
1 *onion, sliced*	*seasoning*
a bouquet garni with plenty of thyme	*red currant jelly*
1 *oz (25 g) butter*	*Forcemeat Balls (page 151)*

Place the hare in a large bowl. Cover with the blood and wine, add the onion and bouquet garni and leave it for at least 24 hours.

When the hare is to be cooked, drain off and retain the liquid. Heat the butter in a frying pan and sautez the hare and onion. Place these together with herbs in a casserole (oven or electric). Stir the flour into the remaining fat and brown. Add the garlic. Gradually stir in the liquid. When it thickens, season to taste, stir in 1 tbs. (15 ml) red currant jelly and pour the sauce over the hare. Cover and cook by day or night. Just before serving, add *Forcemeat Balls*. Serve with more red currant jelly.

Jugged Hare (2)

Medium or cool oven position or electric casserole
Approx. preparation time 15 minutes

This is also a good dish, not quite as rich as the previous recipe but useful when hare joints are available and a whole hare would be too much.

For 2 portions allow:

2 hare joints
2 tbs. (30 ml) flour
¼ tsp. (1·25 ml) salt and a little pepper
1 oz (25 g) butter or dripping
2 rashers of streaky bacon, cut into strips
6 small pickling onions or 1 onion, sliced

½ clove garlic, crushed in salt (optional)
½ bay leaf
2 tsp. (10 ml) chopped parsley
a strip of lemon rind
2 fl. oz (50 ml) port
2 tsp. (10 ml) red currant jelly
¼ beef stock cube

Shake the hare joints in a paper bag with flour, salt and pepper until coated. Heat the fat in a flame-proof casserole or a frying pan and fry the hare and bacon. Remove the hare joints when they begin to brown. Add onion and garlic to the bacon and fry together gently until the onion is soft. Shake in the remaining seasoned flour, stir it into the other ingredients and continue to stir until the flour browns. When using a frying pan, transfer the mixture to a casserole (oven or electric). Add the hare and remaining ingredients and enough water nearly to cover them. Fasten the lid and cook by day or night.

Serve with *Forcemeat Balls* (page 151) and more red currant jelly.

Condensed Soup Casseroles

Oven position depends on meat used, or electric casserole
Approx. preparation time 2 minutes

Of all casseroles these are the simplest to prepare. Certainly they have no connection with haute cuisine – any honour and glory for their creation belong to Mr Heinz and his fraternity. They are, however, delicious and allow for considerable variety.

Just put a harmonizing condensed – not creamed – soup in a closely covered casserole with any chosen lean meat, poultry or game and cook very slowly for 8 hours or longer. A little sherry is a good addition, and some combinations are improved by a teaspoon of red currant jelly. The better the cut of meat, the lower the oven position required.

For 2 portions allow about 3 tbs. (45 ml) of condensed soup.

The number of possible combinations must be considerable. Here are just a few suggestions:

Pea and Ham Soup with pie veal
Mushroom Soup with chicken joints
Mushroom Soup with pork chops
Oxtail Soup with beefsteak
Tomato Soup with lamb chops
Vegetable Soup with pig's kidneys

COLD MEATS

Pressed Beef

(Prepare 12 hours before cooking)
Coolest oven position or electric casserole
Approx. preparation time 5 minutes

This is a good summer dish, either served with salad or in sandwiches. Expensive cuts are not necessary – topside, chuck and rolled flank are good, also brisket for those who like fat.

For a 1½ lb (600 g) piece of beef allow:

1 *clove garlic*	*a few peppercorns*
1 *onion, grated*	1 *clove*
1 *carrot, grated*	2 *tsp. (10 ml) vinegar*
1 *tsp. (5 ml) moist sugar*	*water*
1 *tsp. (5 ml) salt*	2 *level tsp. (10 ml) powdered*
2 *tsp. (10 ml) mixed spice*	*gelatine*

Cut garlic into slivers, and push these into the beef. Put this into a casserole very little larger than the joint. Arrange the vegetables, seasoning and spices round the meat. Add vinegar and enough water just to cover the beef. Store for 12 hours. Cook day or night in a casserole with a tight-fitting lid in oven or transfer to a heated electric casserole.

When tender, lift meat and place it in a closely fitting cake tin or basin.

The Glaze (the same quantity will be sufficient for larger joints). Pour the liquor into a measure. Put the gelatine into a small jug or a cup. Remove any solids from the liquor, and after a few minutes, when the meat juices have sunk to the bottom, pour off the top, leaving ¼ pt (125 ml). Mix a little of this with the gelatine, heat the rest, and when boiling add to the gelatine. Test seasoning, and pour over the meat. Shake gently so that the glaze penetrates into any cracks and crevices. Cover with a plate or saucer. Put weights on this and leave till quite cold before turning out.

Jellied Pork

Medium oven position or electric casserole
Approx. preparation time 4 minutes

This tasty, summer dish from Austria is made with any cut of lean pork and a few pork bones. The weight of the joint must depend on the size of the casserole available.

For a 2–3 lb (800 g–1½ kg) piece of pork and some bones allow:

2 or 3 large onions, sliced	*salt and pepper to taste*
2 or 3 large carrots, sliced	*1 tsp. (5 ml) sugar*
a stick of celery (optional)	*equal quantities of water and*
a little parsley and thyme	*white wine or water and*
a bay leaf	*vinegar sufficient to cover*
a few strips of lemon peel	*the other ingredients*

Salad and garnish for serving:

Lettuce, dressed with a lemon	*cucumber*
French dressing	*peeled grapes*
hard-boiled egg	*cooked peas*
tomato	

Put all the ingredients in a casserole (oven or electric) just large enough to hold them. Cover with a tightly fitting lid and cook by day or night.

When the meat is cooked and really tender, increase the heat so that the stock simmers for a few minutes. Do not let it boil. Place the pork in a deep dish or basin and strain the liquor over it. Cool (quickly) and leave in a refrigerator to allow the jelly to set.

To serve, slice the meat, cut the jelly into small pieces, and arrange on the dressed lettuce. Decorate with the garnishes.

Galantines

(Cook as soon as prepared)
Hot or medium oven position or electric casserole
Approx. pre-cooking preparation time 8 minutes
Approx. post-cooking preparation time 10 minutes

These can be made from a choice of meats and used in various ways – all delicious, attractive and easy to prepare. The choice of meats is :

Beef : any of the cheaper cuts.
Fresh or pickled pork : lean
   belly is good and cheap.
Pie veal and ham or bacon
   (pieces or rashers).
Pie veal and pickled pork : this is
   especially good when the pork
   is inclined to be salty.

Any combination of these meats can be used and the addition of *a little liver* (calf, pig or sheep) makes a creamier galantine.

Cut meat into pieces about 1″ (2–3 cm) cube. Place these in a pudding basin with no seasoning and cover with a firmly tied pudding cloth. Do not use foil. Stand the basin in a pan of boiling water – the water should come halfway up the basin. Cover. Boil for 5 minutes. Immediately put pan in oven or transfer to a heated electric casserole containing boiling water.

After 8 hours or more cooking the meat will be tender and sitting in nice rich gravy. Remove meat and mince it two or three times or liquidize. Replace the minced meat into the warm gravy, and mix thoroughly. Season freely with salt (except with ham, bacon or pickled pork), pepper, garlic salt (optional), tomato, Worcester or soy sauce, or mustard or horseradish sauce (pages 147, 148), or sherry to taste.

While the galantine is still warm and pliable, make it into any of the following dishes :

Galantine Loaf

Freshly made galantine (recipe   *hard-boiled eggs*
   above)   *(optional)*

For a plain galantine : press the warm mixture into a loaf tin. When eggs are to be incorporated : first press a layer of galantine on the bottom of the tin, place the eggs on this, press more of the mixture round the eggs and cover them with the remainder.

Turn out when cold and firm. Serve within 24 hours, or store in a refrigerator or freezer.

Scotch Eggs

Admittedly these lack the crispness of the orthodox fried Scotch Eggs, but they are certainly good and quick to prepare.

Freshly made galantine (recipe   *hard-boiled eggs*
on pages 69 to 70)   *brown breadcrumbs*

Flatten out the warm galantine mixture on a floured working surface. Divide into portions equal in number to the eggs. Place an egg on each portion. Wrap the galantine all round, and roll the ball on the floured surface. Drop the covered eggs, one by one, into a small basin, containing crumbs. Bounce them round and round until they are completely coated. That is all – no further cooking is necessary. Serve within 24 hours, or store in a refrigerator or freezer.

Galantine Meat Pies

These are easy to make with galantine, and are especially good when made with pickled pork and veal.

Freshly made galantine (recipe   *hard-boiled eggs (optional)*
on pages 69 to 70)   *short crust paste*

Press the warm galantine into small individual metal or foil tins. If liked, half a hard-boiled egg may be incorporated in each. Allow the galantine to cool and set. Complete the pies within 24 hours when not stored in a refrigerator or freezer. The method is as follows:

Remove galantine moulds from the tins.

For each mould, roll a small piece of paste into a round large enough to cover the bottom and sides of the mould. Turn the moulds upside down, and brush with water. Lay a round of paste on each, press it and adjust to fit snugly over the bottom and round the sides. Reverse pies, so that the paste can be worked a little higher than the moulds, to form a rim of about ¼" (½ cm).

Make the lids by rolling small balls of paste into rounds, slightly larger than the top of the tins in which the pies were set. Lay these on top of the pies, pressing all the edges together.

Either pin a strip of grease-proof paper round each pie, or return them to the little tins – the latter is the better method for pickled pork galantine, which contains more fat, and will not hold its shape as well as galantines made from leaner meat. Bake in a hot oven until brown.

Ham and Bacon Joints

Oven position according to size of joint; or electric casserole
Approx. preparation time 1 minute

Ham and bacon joints respond well to slow cooking. It is as well to soak joints – other than very mild cures and the 'tender sweet' variety – for 12 to 24 hours before cooking. For any cut of ham or bacon allow:

Cloves (optional)
water or equal quantities of
cider and water

1–2 tbs. (15–30 ml) brown
sugar or treacle

Stick joint with the cloves and place it in a casserole (oven or electric) or stewpan. Almost cover with the liquid and add the sweetening. Cover, and cook by day or night as convenient. A large joint will need a hot oven position. The smaller the joint, the cooler the oven position.

When cooked and really tender, remove the skin. Also take out the bones from joints other than the whole hams. Cool compact cuts in their liquor, but press awkward joints. These will be much easier to carve. Use either a meat press or a cake tin with a loose bottom. With the latter, fit the hot joint snugly into the tin. Reverse the lot onto a plate. Press down the tin bottom and stack on it as many weights as possible.

Tongues (Ox, Calves', Pigs' and Lambs') and Pickled Pork

These can be prepared the same way as ham and bacon joints. For hot *Pickled Pork and Beans*, see page 58.

Ham Loaf

(Soak the ham for 24 hours before cooking)
Medium and hot oven positions
Pre-cooking preparation time approx. 3 minutes
Post-cooking preparation time approx. 8 minutes

This ham loaf, though a genuine economy recipe, is suitable for any occasion. It cuts well and is essentially a cold dish, though slices egged, crumbed and fried in butter or lard make a good hot meal. It is made with knuckles or other ends of ham or bacon cuts that are offered at bargain prices. The amount of meat on knuckles of the same weight does vary, but the following should make a loaf to fill a 1 lb (400 g) bread tin:

a 2 lb (800 g) knuckle

a bay leaf (optional)

1 tbs. (15 ml) black treacle
  (optional)

¼ lb (100 g) split peas

water

1 tsp. (5 ml) made mustard
  (optional)

1 tbs. (15 ml) chopped sweet
  pickles (optional)

Place the soaked ham in a casserole with the water coming about halfway up. Add the bay leaf and treacle. Cover and cook in the oven's medium position by day or night. Put the split peas in a small saucepan with 8 fl. oz (200 ml) boiling water. Cover with a tightly fitting lid and place over heat until the water begins to bubble, then immediately place in the oven's hottest position to cook at the same time as the ham.

When cooked, remove the rind and bone from the ham, cut the flesh and fat into pieces and mix them with the strained peas. Put the lot twice through the mincer. Mix in mustard and pickles and pack the mixture into the loaf tin. Turn out when cold.

Brawn

Medium oven position or large electric casserole
Pre-cooking preparation time approx. 10 minutes
Post-cooking preparation time approx. 15 minutes

Half a pig's head provides a tasty dish and a dozen or so economical portions. Ask the butcher to chop the head into two or more pieces so that it fits snugly into its container. He will take out the eye – you can also present him with the brains, ear and snout, unless they are wanted for a cat.

½ pig's head

2 onions, grated

1 tbs. (15 ml) peppercorns

a blade of mace

6 cloves

a bouquet garni

2 tsp. (10 ml) salt

1 tbs. (15 ml) allspice (optional)

about 1¼ pt (625 ml) water

First blanch the head in a large pan of boiling water for about 3 minutes, then scrape well to remove all the bristles and clean thoroughly. Place in a stewpan with a tightly fitting lid (weighted if pan is shallow) or an electric casserole. Add the other ingredients – the water should almost cover the meat. Cook during the day or night.

When cooked and very tender, remove the flesh from the bones. Return the bones to the liquor and boil on top of the stove while the meat is being prepared. Having removed any gristle and thick skin, cut the meat into ½″ (1 cm) dice and about three parts fill one or more wetted moulds or basins. Strain off the boiled stock, test for seasoning and pour it over the meat, so that it is completely covered. Turn out when cold.

Other dishes that are good served cold are *Sausage Rolls* (page 91), *Sausage Loaf* (page 90), *Jellied Chicken* (pages 92 and 95).

ROASTS

Meat and poultry – all cuts and weights from less than a pound to 4½ lbs (2 kgs) – are really delicious when roasted very, very slowly in an oven or an electric casserole. Shrinkage is negligible, and the flesh becomes tender and juicy, and slices well. The flavour is excellent, with one exception – the best cuts of beef. These only remain rare and retain their distinctive flavour when roasted quickly. On the other hand, cheap cuts of beef, when roasted by the ultra-slow method, though well-done, melt in the mouth.

For roasting in an electric casserole, see page 24.

An oven roast, before slow cooking, should be given 15–30 minutes according to size at setting 400° F., 200° C. or gas mark 6 to seal in juices and ensure death of bacteria.

Meat, to be cooked to perfection, must reach a temperature throughout of 140° F. (60° C.) for underdone beef and 190° F. (88° C.) for pork or poultry. The slow-cooking oven should be within this range. The meat will not dry up or be more than slightly overcooked however long it is kept in the oven, as it cannot get hotter than the oven itself. Should the oven not be quite hot enough, all that is needed is a longer spell in a hotter oven (about 350° F., 180° C. or gas mark 4) than is normally required for the final browning. The only way to ascertain the exact temperature of roasts is with a meat thermometer (see page 17). The thermometer is pushed into the thickest part of the meat – it must not rest on a bone – and is left there to register its cooking progress. Of course joints can be roasted without meat thermometers but not with the same assurance.

It is most important to make sure that frozen meat or poultry is completely thawed before it is slow cooked.

Hot roasts should be served as soon as cooked; they are never at their best when reheated.

Roasts for the evening meal should cook during the day in the oven's coolest or medium position or in an electric casserole. Roasts for the mid-day meal can begin slow roasting the night before in the oven's coolest position, provided this is cool enough, or early that morning in the oven's medium or hottest position, or in an electric casserole. Allow sufficient time to give joints (especially pork or poultry) a spell of hotter treatment; for chops or cutlets place under grill for final browning.

Only the very leanest of joints need brushing with olive oil. Place thin slices of streaky bacon on the breast of birds other than geese and ducks.

Wrap oven roasts in cooking film * or aluminium foil with the covering overlapping on top of the meat. When a meat thermometer is used this can be pushed through the covering. Wrap chops and cutlets in pairs for daylong cooking and individually for morning cooking.

Oven roasts should be put on racks, and not directly on the meat tin, so that the hot air can circulate freely. Racks from grill pans, poaching rings and pastry cutters can be used.

To brown meat remove covering, taking care that the trapped meat juices run into the meat tin. Scrape off any meat essence that adheres to the covering. The meat juices and essence form the base of the gravy and should not be submitted to greater heat. Therefore set it aside after pouring off any surplus fat. Place the roast in a clean tin and brown for a short spell in a hotter oven. The one disadvantage is that the fat, though nicely browned, will not be really crisp. Many people will not mind, as they spurn all fat, however delicious. But those who do enjoy fat – pork crackling in particular – and crisp, brown birds, need not be deprived if either of the following methods is used :

1) This is good for all joints with skin-covered fat and for poultry, especially ducks and geese. Half to three-quarters of an hour before serving, remove the roast from cool oven and place, unwrapped, on a clean tin and leave it on top of the cooker. Raise oven temperature to very hot. (This is a good opportunity to roast pressure-cooked or parboiled potatoes and bake Yorkshire pudding, pies and tarts.) About 15 minutes before the meal, hold the roast under a cold running tap for a few

* The modern transparent cooking film is far better than aluminium foil for ultra-slow roasting. It ensures crisper and browner results. L O O K! cooking film, marketed by Terinex Ltd of St Albans, Herts, is now obtainable at most large stores.

seconds. Return it to the tin and immediately place in the hot oven's hottest position, skin, crackling or breast uppermost.

2) This method is good for small joints and pork chops. About ½ hour before serving, cut off skin or crackling with ⅙" to ¼" (⅓ cm to ¼ cm) of fat and place it under a very slow grill.

Stuffed Roasts

Except in the case of that economical and delicious dish, stuffed rolled boned breast of lamb (page 151), it is recommended that the stuffing for slow-roasted meat and poultry (page 151) should be cooked separately.

Gravy

Place in a small casserole or stewpan any bones removed from joints, or the neck, giblets, heart and liver from birds. Cover with water, add salt and pepper and, if liked, a little grated onion. Fasten the lid and cook at the same time as the roast in any convenient oven position or on the hob. This provides stock for the gravy.

To make gravy: add enough flour to the fat and juices in the roasting tin or electric casserole to absorb the fat. Mix well and gradually stir in stock or water to make sufficient gravy of the preferred consistency. Test the seasoning. Place over gentle heat and stir until the gravy thickens.

MORE MEAT DISHES

Steak and Kidney Pudding

Made from *Casseroled Steak and Kidney*, 1 or 2 (pages 40 to 42).
Approx. preparation time 25 minutes

This is not the traditional pudding, as the crust is only on the top – an advantage to many who, with an eye on their figures, are glad to cut down on carbohydrate.

The pudding is made either as soon as the steak and kidney is cooked, or after it has been stored. In both cases it must be in a flame-proof casserole or stewpan. The size of the container is important. It must be just large enough for the mixture to come within 3″ to 1½″ (7½ cm–4 cm) from the top of the container. While preparing the crust, either keep the meat hot or reheat it over a gentle heat. It should be just boiling when the crust is added.

The Crust

For 2–4 portions allow :

8 fl. oz (200 ml) finely grated fresh breadcrumbs	seasoning
4 tbs. (60 ml) shredded suet	½ tsp. (2·5 ml) mixed herbs (optional)
6 tbs (90 ml) self-raising flour	a little cold water

Mix the dry ingredients in a mixing bowl, and slowly dribble the water round the rim, working it into the mixture with a pliable knife or a fork to make a firm dough. Knead this into a ball. Remove the casserole or pan lid, and, if it will stand, place it handle down on a working surface, otherwise perch it on a small basin or a jam jar. Dredge the lid with flour, and place the dough on it. Work this with floured hands until it almost fits the lid. The meat should now be boiling very gently. Drop the crust carefully from the lid into the pan. Cover closely and continue cooking over a gentle heat for 1/4 hour.

Steak and Kidney Pie

Made from *Casseroled Steak and Kidney 1 or 2* (pages 40 to 42).
Preparation time depends on whether or not pastry is available.

Turn the cooked steak and kidney (newly cooked or thawed) into a pie dish. The dish must be just large enough to accommodate the mixture and a pie crust holder. The pastry must not be applied until the meat is cold. When short crust or rough puff pastry is used, the pie can be covered a day or so before baking, but puff pastry must be put on and baked just before serving unless stored in the freezer. •

Hamburgers

Medium or cool oven position or electric casserole
Approx. preparation time 5 minutes
For 2 portions allow:

1 *slice crustless bread*	1 *small onion, grated*
4" × 2½" × ½"	2 tsp. (10 ml) *chopped parsley*
(10 cm × 6 cm × 1 cm)	½ tsp. (2·5 ml) *salt and a little*
2 *fl. oz (50 ml) either boiling*	*pepper*
stock or boiling water and ¼	1 *small egg*
beef stock cube	*browned breadcrumbs*
½ lb (200 g) *best minced beef*	

Place the bread on a large plate. When stock is not available, crumble the stock cube into a measure and add the boiling water. Pour this or the boiling stock over the bread, and mash with a fork. Add meat, onion, parsley and seasoning. Mix well. Beat the egg and blend with other ingredients. Divide mixture into two portions. Cut 2 pieces of foil about 8" x 10" (20 cm x 25 cm), and sprinkle crumbs onto the centre of each piece. Place the hamburgers on top of the crumbs, sprinkle well with more crumbs and wrap them in the foil.

Slow cook, resting on a grid or poaching or cutting rings, in a small roasting tin or an electric casserole with a little water. When the hamburgers have had their spell of day or night cooking, lift them carefully from the foil onto an oven dish, and, if to be served immediately, keep warm in the oven while the sauce is made.

The Sauce

A little water, stock or wine   (page 137) or the ready-made
2 tsp. (10 ml) tomato sauce   variety (optional)

Scrape all the thick meat and egg juices from the foil into the meat tin or a small pan. Add enough of the chosen liquid to dilute and make sufficient sauce. Add the tomato sauce, if you are using it. Place the tin or pan over a very gentle heat and stir with a wooden spoon until the mixture is well blended. Pour the sauce over the hamburgers and either serve, or store and reheat as required.

Moussaka

Medium or cool oven position
Approx. preparation time 15 minutes

This delicious dish of Greek origin can be reheated, but is at its best cooked all day and served the same evening.

L.I.T.C. – 5

For 4 portions allow:

1 lb (400 g) best minced beef	1 large onion, sliced
2 tbs. (30 ml) olive oil, butter or margarine	1 large tomato, skinned and sliced, or 1 tsp. (5 ml) tomato purée
2 tsp. (10 ml) flour	
1 tbs. (15 ml) water or white wine	2 tbs. (30 ml) chopped parsley
	salt and pepper to taste
a choice of: ¼ lb (100 g) mushrooms, sliced, or 1 aubergine, sliced unpeeled, or 1 green pepper, seeded and sliced	3–4 oz (75–100 g) cheese, finely grated
	2 eggs
	1 tsp. (5 ml) dry mustard
	½ pt (250 ml) milk

Place the mince in a flame-proof casserole or a frying pan, and sautez in half the fat over a gentle heat. When the meat changes colour, stir in the flour and liquid. Turn the mixture onto a plate. Put the remaining fat into a casserole or pan and sautez the vegetables, stirring them with a wooden spoon until the onion becomes clear. Remove from heat and stir in the mince, tomato purée (when chosen), parsley and seasoning. Mix well, and, when using a frying pan, transfer the mixture to an oven dish. Press it down firmly – it should not be higher than an inch (2–3 cm) from the top of the container. Spread the cheese evenly over the top. Beat the eggs in a small basin with the mustard. Add the milk and whisk. Pour the egg mixture over the cheese and immediately place in the oven.

This dish can be prepared in advance, provided the egg and milk mixture is not added until the moussaka is about to go into the oven.

Bobotie

Medium oven position or electric casserole
Approx. preparation time 12 minutes

A tasty South African dish, adapted to ultra-slow cooking.
For 3 portions allow:

1 thick slice of crustless bread	¼ tsp. (1·25 ml) salt and a little pepper
8 fl. oz (200 ml) hot milk	
½ oz (12·5 g) butter or margarine	1 tsp. (5 ml) chopped parsley
1 onion, sliced	1 tbs. (15 ml) lemon juice or vinegar
½ lb (200 g) best minced beef	1 tbs. (15 ml) chopped salted peanuts
1 heaped tbs. (20 ml) curry powder	
1 tsp. (5 ml) brown sugar	a little nutmeg (optional)
	2 eggs

Place the bread in a mixing bowl and pour the milk over it. Melt the fat in a small pan, and cook the onion until it is soft. Strain the milk off the bread into a basin and set aside. Mash the sodden bread with a fork, and work into it all the other ingredients except one of the eggs and the milk. Turn the mixture into a greased dish and pack it firmly. Beat the second egg into the strained milk, pour this over the meat mixture. Immediately place in the oven or heated electric casserole. For latter, see section on baking, page 24.

This dish can be prepared in advance, but the well-beaten egg and milk must not be added until the Bobotie is about to be cooked.

Bobotie is nice served with chutney, boiled or fried rice, or creamed potato. *Fried Rice* (page 126) and *Creamed Potato* (page 104) can be cooked at the same time as the Bobotie.

This dish can also be made with minced cooked meat – the Boers recommend cold lamb or mutton.

Ox Liver and Bacon with Onion and Apple Stuffing

Medium or cool oven position or electric casserole
Approx. preparation time 15 minutes
An excellent and economical dish.

For 3–4 portions allow:

½ lb (200 g) ox liver	1½ oz (37.5 g) moist brown
3 tbs. (45 ml) stock or water	sugar (less if preferred)
salt and pepper	¼ pt (125 ml) fresh bread-
2 oz (50 g) rindless bacon pieces	crumbs
1 medium onion, finely sliced	2 oz (50 g) rindless streaky
1 large cooking apple, diced	bacon rashers, sliced No. 4

Wash the liver well in warm water, remove any tubes, fat and skin. Cut into thin slices. Lay these in a greased shallow oven dish. Add the liquid and seasoning. Cut up the bacon pieces and place them in a medium-sized heavy saucepan. Cover, and place over very gentle heat. Cook until the bacon is crisp and has exuded plenty of fat. Add the onion and cook a further few minutes before adding the apple. Still covered, continue to cook until the apple is mushy. Remove pan from heat and stir in the breadcrumbs and sugar. Spread the stuffing evenly over the liver, making sure that it is completely covered. Lay the rashers on top of the stuffing. Cook in oven or transfer covered liver and liquid to a greased, heated electric casserole, or store and cook later.

Veal Cooked with Mushrooms

Coolest oven position or electric casserole
Approx. preparation time 2 minutes per portion
   A delicious yet simple party dish made in two stages.
Stage 1. This is carried out either on the day of the party, or in advance and stored in the refrigerator or freezer.
For each portion allow:

about 5 oz (125 g) veal escalope	salt and pepper
1 oz (25 g) button mushrooms	¼ oz (6.25 g) butter

Cut a piece of foil for each escalope – large enough to wrap round loosely. Rub both sides of meat with salt and pepper and spread with butter. Leave mushrooms whole, but slice any stalks. Place ½ oz (2·5 g) mushrooms on each piece of foil with an escalope on top, covered with the other ½ oz (2·5 g) mushrooms. Enclose the lot in the foil. Rest the parcels on a rack or poaching rings placed in a baking tin or electric casserole, the latter with a little water. Slow cook. The escalopes should be cooked in well under 8 hours.

Stage 2. This is carried out within an hour or so of the party and, if Stage 1 has been stored, the parcels must first be re-heated. For each parcel allow:

¼ tsp. (1·25 ml) *cornflour*   1 tbs. (15 ml) *chopped parsley*
1 tbs. (15 ml) *white wine*   ½ slice *lemon*
1 tbs. (15 ml) *cream or top of*
  the milk

Unwrap the warm parcels onto the hot meat tin or a frying pan, ensuring meat and mushroom juices are scraped off the foil. Carefully lift escalopes on to a heated serving dish with a cover and keep warm. Put cornflour in a cup, stir in the wine and add mixture to the mushrooms and juices. Stir well and cook over gentle heat until sauce thickens. Add cream and any necessary seasoning. Pour hot sauce round the escalopes. Keep dish covered until just before serving, then sprinkle with parsley and lay a slice of lemon on each escalope.

Crumbed Cutlet Ragout

Medium or cool oven position or electric casserole
Approx. preparation time 10 minutes

For 2 portions allow:

4 best end lamb or mutton cutlets about 1/3″ (1 cm) thick	1 carrot, sliced
1 tbs. (15 ml) flour	1/2 clove garlic, crushed in salt (optional)
1/4 tsp. (1·25 ml) salt and a little pepper	1 tbs. (15 ml) barley
1/2 oz (12·5 g) butter and 1/2 tsp. (2·5 ml) olive oil	6 fl. oz (150 ml) stock or water and 1/4 stock cube
1 onion, sliced	1 tsp. (5 ml) mushroom ketchup
	a sprig of rosemary or thyme (optional)

For topping prior to serving: finely grated fresh breadcrumbs.

Remove bones and most of the fat from cutlets. Curl tails round meat and fasten with cocktail sticks. Shake meat in a bag with seasoned flour. Heat fats in a flame-proof casserole or a pan. Brown cutlets on both sides. Remove sticks and set meat aside. Add vegetables and the flour left in the bag to fat. Stir and cook for about 2 minutes. Remove from heat. When using a pan, transfer mixture either to an oven casserole or a slow-cooking electric casserole. Add remaining ingredients and bed cutlets into the vegetables. Cover and cook or store and cook later.

When cooked, after removing herbs, sprinkle top with crumbs, sufficient to absorb fat. Carefully transfer ragout to a shallow oven-proof dish. To serve immediately, place under a grill to brown and crispen the crumbs. To store: chill or freeze, and before serving, heat and brown cutlets in a hot oven.

Squab Pie

(Day cooking. Do not reheat)

Medium or cool oven position

Approx. preparation time 15 minutes

This is an unusual tasty recipe from New Zealand.

For 2 portions allow:

2 trimmed lamb chops	1 medium cooking apple,
2 tsp. (10 ml) flour	peeled, cored and sliced
½ tsp. (2·5 ml) salt	½ tsp. (2·5 ml) moist brown
¼ tsp. (1·25 ml) pepper	sugar
½ oz (12·5 g) dripping or	¼ pt (125 ml) stock or water
butter	slices of bread, ½" (1 cm) thick,
1 large onion, sliced	buttered and crusts removed

Shake chops in a paper bag with the flour and seasoning. Heat fat in a frying pan, brown the chops and set them aside on a plate. Fry the onions until clear, then add the apple and, with a wooden spoon, stir in the rest of the seasoned flour from the bag. Cook for a further two minutes. Remove from heat. Choose a covered oven dish just large enough to hold the chops, side by side. Put a layer of onion and apple on the bottom, then the chops, and cover these with the rest of the onion and apple. Sprinkle on the sugar, and pour the liquid round the side of the dish. Cover the top completely with buttered bread, buttered side uppermost, and press down firmly. Cover. Cook throughout the day, or cool rapidly, store in refrigerator and cook when required. A short time before serving, remove the cover and brown the bread under a grill. Either serve at once or return the pie, still uncovered, to the oven to keep warm.

Pork Chops and Apple

(Do not reheat)

Hot or medium oven position for evening meal; or electric casserole

Coolest oven position for mid-day meal if cooked overnight

Approx. preparation time 5 minutes

These chops are treated like joints. They must be cooked during the day for a meal that evening. When wanted for lunch, they come to no harm if they are put in the oven the previous night or as suggested on page 76.

For 2 chops allow :

1 tsp. (5 ml) made mustard   a little moist brown sugar
   (optional)   1 large cooking apple

Trim chops, removing most of the fat. Spread mustard on both sides. Peel the apples, core and slice into thin rings.

When preparing for an evening meal : cut two pieces of foil, large enough to wrap each chop. Lay a quarter of the apple rings in the centre of each piece, and fill about three of the holes with sugar. Put a chop on top, covered with the rest of the apple, also with a little sugar in the holes. Wrap these up and place in a baking tin or an electric casserole with a little water, resting the parcels on a rack or poaching rings. Cook throughout the day, or store and cook the next day.

When preparing for a mid-day meal : the chops are cooked in pairs, one on top of the other. Cut a piece of foil large enough for this purpose. Lay the chops on this with sugared apple rings underneath, between and on top of them. Place the wrapped chops on a grid over the tin or in an electric casserole. Put in the oven the evening before serving or in an electric casserole set high that morning.

Just before the meal allow the gravy to escape from the foil into the tin, where it can, if liked, be thickened with a little cornflour mixed with a tablespoon of milk, stock, wine or water. The chops will be cooked and succulent, but nevertheless they should be given a brief spell under the grill.

GAMMON RASHERS

These are always a good buy and, when cooked very slowly, are sure to be tender and luscious. A rasher not less than ½″ (1 cm) thick should provide two medium-sized portions.

Those who do not like their ham too salty can soak the rashers, especially when smoked, for up to 12 hours in water or for about 20 minutes in milk. Before cooking, remove the rind, snick fat in several places and if soaked, dry the rasher thoroughly with a cloth or absorbent paper, before cooking.

Gammon rasher recipes are better not reheated. They should therefore be cooked the day of serving.

Gammon Rasher with Tomato and Cheese

Hot or medium oven position or electric casserole
Approx. preparation time 3 minutes
For 1 gammon rasher allow :

a small tin of tomatoes *about ¼lb (100 g) cheese*

Place the prepared rasher in a baking dish or electric casserole, pour over the tomatoes and completely cover with the cheese, either grated or cut into thin slices.

Gammon Rasher Cooked in Sauce

Medium or cool oven position or electric casserole
Approx. preparation time 2 minutes
For 1 gammon rasher allow :

3 tbs. (45 ml) either: Mustard Sauce (page 147) or Tomato Sauce (page 137) or Condensed Soup (page 66).

Cook the rasher in a covered shallow oven container or an electric casserole with the chosen sauce.

Fried Ham Loaf Slices

Page 73.

Sausage Loaf

Medium or cool oven position or electric casserole
Approx. preparation time 20 minutes

This dish can be served hot but is even better cold; it slices
well, is good with salad or in sandwiches and is useful for
picnics. For 2 portions allow :

1½ oz (37.5 g) chopped bacon	¼ pt (125 ml) fresh bread-
1 medium onion, finely sliced	crumbs
1 large cooking apple, diced	1 tbs. (15 ml) moist brown
browned breadcrumbs	sugar
½ lb (200 g) pork sausage meat	¾ tsp. (3.75 ml) made mustard

Put the bacon into a heavy, medium-sized saucepan over
gentle heat. Cover, and cook until it is crisp and has exuded
plenty of fat. Add the onion and cook for a further few
minutes, then add the apple. Still covered, continue to cook
until the apple becomes mushy. Meanwhile grease a 1 lb
(400 g) loaf tin or foil pie dish and coat it well with browned
breadcrumbs. When the apples are cooked, remove pan from
heat, and stir in the remaining ingredients. Mix well, and
transfer mixture to the prepared tin. Pack firmly, and sprinkle
more browned crumbs over the top of the loaf, which is now
ready for the slow cooking when required. For cooking in an
electric casserole, see section on baking, page 24.

When cooked, pour off any fat, turn out the loaf, and
sprinkle again with crumbs.

Hot sausage loaf is good served with tomato sauce, either
home-made (page 137) or from a bottle. The home-made sauce
should be heated.

Sausage Rolls

Hot or medium oven position
Approx. preparation time 5 minutes
These are made with bread instead of the usual pastry.
They are delightfully crisp and crunchy, and good hot or
cold.
For 8 sausage rolls allow:

½ lb (200 g) *skinless sausages*
1 tsp. (5 ml) *made mustard*
  (optional)
1 oz (25 g) *butter or margarine*

3 fl. oz (75 ml) *milk*
8 slices *crustless bread, less*
than ¼″ (½ cm) thick

Spread the sausages with mustard. Put the fat and milk in
a small pan over gentle heat. When the fat has melted, beat
well and pour a little of the mixture onto a plate. Place a
slice of bread in this and return pan to the heat. Roll a
sausage in the partially soaked bread. When all the sausages
are enveloped, pack them firmly into a baking tin and cook
by day or night.

Stuffed Peppers

(Day cooking. Do not reheat)
Medium oven position or electric casserole
Approx. preparation time 7 minutes
For 2 portions allow:

1 or 2 rashers of *streaky bacon,*
  cut into small pieces
2 medium-sized *red or green*
  peppers
1 onion, *shredded*

½ lb (200 g) *sausage meat*
1 tbs. (15 ml) *chopped parsley*
salt and pepper *to taste*
browned breadcrumbs
a little butter

Place the bacon in a frying pan over gentle heat. Cut
peppers in half lengthwise. Remove core and seeds, taking

care not to break the peppers. When the bacon has exuded
sufficient fat, fry the onion until soft. Remove pan from heat
and work the sausage, parsley and seasoning into onion mixture. Fill peppers with this stuffing. Sprinkle with crumbs
and dot with butter. Place the peppers in a well-greased oven
dish or electric casserole. Cover with buttered paper and slow
cook.

Three Good Chicken Party Dishes:
Chicken à la King, Chicken à la Crème and
Jellied Chicken

The first two dishes are hot and the third cold. Either
boiling or roasting birds can be used. The dishes are prepared
in two stages – the first is the same for the three recipes and
must be completed well in advance of the party, especially
for *Jellied Chicken*. The chicken must be quite cold for the
second stage of all three recipes.

Stage 1. Hot or medium oven position for boilers and medium
or cool position for roasters, or electric casserole
Approx. preparation time 3 minutes
Allow :

a chicken – weight according to specific recipe	*salt*
	a few peppercorns
sufficient stock or water almost to cover the bird	*¼ or ½ lb (100 or 200 g) mushrooms (according to recipe)*
a small onion, sliced	
a carrot, sliced	

If possible cook the bird whole. Cut off the necessary limbs
only if the bird will not fit into the largest available casserole
or stewpan. Place the chicken together with neck, giblets,
and the other ingredients (except the mushrooms) in the container. Cover and cook by day or night as convenient. Put

the mushrooms in a small container and cook them at the
same time either according to recipe on page 103, or with a
little butter over a gentle heat. A boiling fowl may need
longer than 8 hours; leave it until really tender.

When cooked, take out the chicken oddments, the vegetables (these can be used for soup) and the peppercorns.
Leave the bird, breast down, in its liquor. Cool rapidly and
store in refrigerator. *Stage 2 for Chicken à la King* and
Chicken à la Crème is carried out on the day the dish is to
be eaten. *Stage 2 for Jellied Chicken* should be carried out a
day or two before it is needed. Also store the cooked mushrooms. When *Jellied Chicken* is to be made the mushroom
liquor should be incorporated into the chicken liquor.

Chicken à la King (Stage 2)

Approx. preparation time 10 minutes

Once prepared, this dish can be kept hot for an hour or so
in a very cool oven without being spoiled.

For 4 portions allow:

a 3 lb (1½ kg) *chicken and* ½ lb (200 g) *mushrooms, both cooked as in Stage 1*	8 fl. oz (200 ml) *chicken stock (taken from the bottom of the container)*
a 6 oz (150 g) *tin of pimentos (sweet red peppers)*	1 egg yolk
1oz (25 g) *chicken fat (if not enough make up quantity with butter)*	seasoning
2 tbs. (30 ml) flour	10 almonds, blanched and slivered (optional)
	1 tbs. (15 ml) sherry (optional)

Remove the skin from the chicken, carve off the flesh
and dice. Strain and slice the mushrooms and pimentos.
Melt fat in a flame-proof casserole or a saucepan. Add flour
and stir with a wooden spoon. Cook for a minute or so before
gradually adding the stock, together with mushroom and

pimento liquor, stirring continually until the sauce thickens and begins to boil. Add the chicken, mushrooms and pimentos. Lower heat, add the egg yolk and allow mixture to thicken without boiling. Season to taste, and add almonds and sherry. Keep warm. *Baked Creamed Potatoes* (page 104) or *Rice Balls* (page 127) go well with this dish. The potato (if slow cooked) and the rice balls should be cooked during Stage 1.

Chicken à la Crème (Stage 2)

Approx. preparation time 10 minutes
For 4 portions allow:

a 3 lb (1½ kg) chicken and ¼ lb (100 g) mushrooms both cooked as in Stage 1	*1 oz (25 g) butter*
4 slices of cooked ham	*1½ tbs. (22·5 ml) flour*
¼ pt (125 ml) hot chicken stock	*4 fl. oz (100 ml) single cream or milk*
16 grapes, peeled and seeded, or 16 green olives, stoned and sliced	*4 fl. oz (100 ml) chicken stock taken from the bottom of the container*
	1 tbs. (15 ml) chopped parsley seasoning

Skin the chicken and carefully carve all the flesh off the bones. Place this, together with the ham in a warm dish, separating the slices of breast, slices of leg and scrappy pieces. Pour over the ¼ pt (125 ml) hot stock. Cover and leave in a very cool oven. Strain the mushrooms and put them in a small container with the prepared grapes or olives; cover and place in the oven with the chicken. Melt the butter in a small saucepan. Stir in the flour with a wooden spoon, and, when blended, gradually add the liquids including the mushroom liquor, stirring continuously until the sauce thickens. Add the parsley and check for seasoning, adding more if required. Cover the pan and leave in the oven where it will come to no harm for an hour or so. Shortly before the meal, arrange the chicken and ham in portions on a hot serving dish – first a slice of ham, then a layer of scrappy bits, with slices of breast and leg on top. Pour the sauce over these portions and garnish with mushrooms and grapes or olives.

Jellied Chicken (Stage 2)

Preparation time, including the cooling, but not setting, of the jelly, about 1 hour

This is an excellent and fairly economical cold party dish. For 8 portions allow:

a 3½–4 lb (1¾–2 kg) chicken and ¼ lb (100 g) mushrooms, both cooked as in Stage 1
¾ lb (300 g) cooked ham or bacon *
1½ tbs. (22·5 ml) gelatine
2 fl. oz (50 ml) cold water
¾ pt (375 ml) chicken liquor

rind and juice ½ lemon
2 fl. oz (50 ml) sherry
1½ tsp. (7·5 ml) sugar
3 heaped tbs. (60 ml) chopped pineapple pieces
a hard-boiled egg
some cooked green peas or sliced stuffed olives

Put the gelatine and water in a small basin and allow to soak. Pour the chicken liquor into a saucepan, add the lemon rind and bring to the boil. Pour a little boiling liquor over the soaked gelatine, stir until the gelatine dissolves, then tip it back into the pan. Reheat to boiling point, remove from heat and add the lemon juice, sherry and sugar. Skim off any froth, add necessary seasoning and pour jelly into a jug. Set aside to cool.

Skin the chicken. Carefully carve flesh from bones in as few pieces as possible – the breast not sliced but cut from the breast bone in two sections. Put the ham twice through a mincer. Cut up the mushrooms and mix them with the pine-

* A small joint of ham or bacon (page 72) can be cooked during Stage 1 of the chicken preparation.

apple into the minced ham. Slice the egg. Place the egg, the chicken, the ham mixture and the peas or olives on separate dishes. As soon as the jelly is cold but not set, mix about a quarter of it with the ham mixture, and pour sufficient over the other ingredients, to coat them. Rinse a 2 lb (800 g) loaf tin in cold water. Pour in a little jelly and arrange the egg and peas or olives attractively on the bottom. Lean the breast sections against the tin's longer sides and anchor them with a little ham mixture. Fill up the tin with alternate layers of chicken and ham, finishing with chicken and a thin layer of jelly. Press down firmly. With a broad knife, slightly ease the sides of the mould away from the tin and pour round the rest of the jelly. Leave in the tin until completely set.

Meat and Egg Rechauffé

(Day cooking only. Do not reheat)
Medium oven position; or electric casserole (*high*, 1½–2 hours)
Approx. preparation time 7 minutes
For 2 portions allow:

4 thin slices crustless bread	*salt and pepper to taste*
chutney (optional)	*½ pt (250 ml) milk*
minced cooked meat	*1 oz (25 g) grated cheese*
1 egg	*browned breadcrumbs*
½ tsp. (2.5 ml) mustard	

Spread the bread with chutney and mince, and make into sandwiches. Place these in a greased oven dish. Beat the egg with the mustard. Add seasoning and milk. Whisk well until blended, and pour over the sandwiches. Sprinkle with crumbs, spread the cheese on top and place in the oven or electric casserole, or store and cook the next day. For cooking in an electric casserole, see section on baking, page 24.

Vegetables

The recipes in this section are for those vegetables that are delicious when cooked very slowly. Green vegetables, peas, beans and cauliflower do not comply, and slow cooking is not for them. However, these vegetables can always be included in an otherwise slowly cooked menu, since they take only a little longer to cook than is needed to set the table.

Buttered Carrots

(Cook as soon as prepared)
Medium or cool oven position or electric casserole
Approx. preparation time 5 minutes
 These are good as a hot vegetable or as a salad.
For 2 portions allow:

¾ lb (300 g) carrots	¼ tsp. (1·25 ml) sugar
½ oz (12·5 g) butter	2 tsp. (10 ml) top of milk
¼ tsp. (1·25 ml) salt	2 tsp. (10 ml) chopped parsley

 Peel or scrape carrots and slice them into long thin strips. Melt the butter in a small pan with a well-fitting lid, add the carrots, cover and cook over gentle heat for two to three minutes. Shake the pan now and then. Add seasoning and top of milk. Allow to simmer for another minute, then immediately place in oven or transfer to heated electric casserole.
 When cooked, add the parsley, and serve at once, or mix

a little French dressing into the hot carrots and serve cold as a salad.

Creamed Parsnips, Turnips or Swedes

Medium or cool oven position or electric casserole
Approx. preparation time 10 minutes
For 3–4 portions allow :

1 lb (400 g) vegetables, washed, scraped or peeled and cut into thin slices	½ oz (12·5 g) butter or margarine
a small onion, shredded	2 tsp. (10 ml) flour
¼ pt (125 ml) stock or water	salt and pepper to taste
¼ pt (125 ml) milk	1 tbs. (15 ml) chopped parsley (optional)

Place the sliced vegetables, the onion and liquid in a saucepan and simmer for about 5 minutes. Strain, retaining the liquor. Place the vegetables in a casserole. Melt fat in the pan. Stir in the flour and seasoning. Gradually add the liquor. Cook gently, stirring continuously until the sauce thickens. Check for seasoning, add the parsley, and pour the sauce over the vegetables. Mix well. Cover and cook by day or night. These slowly cooked root vegetables freeze well.

Creamed Leeks, Celery, Chicory or Onions

Medium or cool oven position or electric casserole
Approx. preparation time 10 minutes
   These four vegetables are delicious when cooked slowly in a sauce, and at least one of them will be in season throughout the year. All can be frozen.
For 2 portions allow :

½ lb (200 g) vegetables	½ oz (12·5 g) butter or margarine
3 fl. oz (75 ml) water	
milk	1 tbs. (15 ml) flour
	salt and pepper to taste

Wash and prepare the vegetables:

Leeks: cut in two lengthwise, then slice each half into 2" (5 cm) pieces.

Celery: cut sticks into 3" (7·8 cm) lengths.

Chicory: cut into two lengthwise.

Onions: cut vertically into halves or quarters.

Boil the vegetables in the water for two minutes. Strain the liquid into a measure. Place the vegetables in a casserole (either oven or electric) with a tight-fitting lid. Add sufficient milk to bring the vegetable liquor up to 6 fl. oz (150 ml). Melt the fat in the pan. Stir in the flour and gradually add the liquid. Continue to stir over the gentle heat until the sauce thickens. Season to taste, pour over the vegetables and mix well. Cook during the day or night as convenient.

Marrow Casserole

Medium or cool oven position or electric casserole
Approx. preparation time 8 minutes
For 2–3 portions allow:

¾ lb (300 g) peeled, seeded marrow	1 onion, grated
	1 oz (25 g) butter
1 tbs. (15 ml) seasoned flour	2 fl. oz (50 ml) milk

Cut marrow into 2" (5 cm) cubes. Shake in a bag with seasoned flour. Melt the butter in a flame-proof casserole or stewpan over gentle heat. Add the flour-covered marrow and the onion. Cook for a few minutes. Add the milk and bring to the boil. Cover and immediately place in a casserole (oven or electric), or store and cook later. If it has been stored, the dish should be reheated on the hob before it is slow cooked. This dish freezes well – a good way to preserve surplus marrow.

Onion in Sago Sauce

(Cook as soon as prepared)
Hot or medium oven position or electric casserole
Approx. preparation time 5 minutes
For 2 portions allow:

2 large Spanish onions, cut vertically in quarters	½ oz (12·5 g) butter or margarine
4 fl. oz (100 ml) water	½ tsp. (2·5 ml) salt
4 fl. oz (100 ml) milk	¼ tsp. (1·25 ml) pepper
1 tbs. (15 ml) sago	

Boil the onions in the water for 2 minutes in a flame-proof casserole or saucepan with a well-fitting lid. Add other ingredients and bring to the boil again. Stir well, cover. Immediately place in the oven or transfer to a heated electric casserole.

Onion Ragout

Hot or medium oven position or electric casserole
Approx. preparation time 6 minutes
For 2–3 portions allow:

½ oz (12·5 g) butter or margarine	¼ tsp. (1·25 ml) each salt and pepper
1 lb (400 g) onions, sliced	2 tbs. (30 ml) dry white wine, dry cider or water
¼ lb (100 g) tomatoes, skinned and sliced	1 clove
	½ a bay leaf

Heat fat over gentle heat in a flame-proof casserole or pan with a well-fitting lid. Cook the onion until clear. Add the tomato and stir it into the fat with a wooden spoon. Add other ingredients. Cover and cook immediately, or store and cook later. If stored, the dish should be reheated on the hot plate before being placed in the oven or transferred to an electric casserole.

This dish also makes a base for savouries (page 125). It freezes well.

Ratatouille

Hot or medium oven position or electric casserole
Approx. preparation time 15 minutes

This vegetable stew is very popular in the south of France. The recipe can be varied to taste by increasing or decreasing the quantity of any of the given vegetables.

For 4–5 portions allow:

3 tbs. (45 ml) olive oil
3 medium onions, sliced
½ lb (200 g) marrow, peeled
   and sliced, or courgettes,
   sliced unpeeled
1 aubergine, sliced unpeeled

2 green or red peppers, seeds
   removed, then sliced
2 tomatoes, skinned and sliced
2 cloves garlic, crushed in salt
½ tsp. (2·5 ml) salt
¼ tsp. (1·25 ml) freshly ground
   black pepper

Heat the oil over gentle heat in a flame-proof casserole or stewpan. Cook the onion until it begins to soften. Add marrow or courgettes, aubergine and peppers. Cook for a further five minutes before adding the remaining ingredients. Cover. Immediately place in oven or transfer to electric casserole, or store and reheat on hob before cooking.

When cooked, the vegetables should be very soft and have absorbed the oil. This dish reheats well – in fact, it improves with reheating – and can be frozen.

German Red Cabbage

Medium or cool oven position or electric casserole
Approx. preparation time 8 minutes

For 3–4 portions allow:

1 lb (400 g) red cabbage, shredded	1 oz (25 g) melted butter or lard
boiling water	½ tsp. (2·5 ml) ground caraway seed (optional)
2 tsp. (10 ml) vinegar	salt
2 tsp. (10 ml) grated onion	2½ fl. oz (62·5 ml) water
1 medium-sized cooking apple, peeled and chopped	1 tbs. (15 ml) sugar
	a small raw potato (optional)

Scald the cabbage in boiling water. Drain and place in a flame-proof casserole or stewpan and immediately stir in the vinegar. Place over gentle heat. Add fat, onion, apple and seasoning. Mix well and cook a few minutes. Add the water. Cover. Either place in the oven or transfer to an electric casserole, or store and reheat on the hob before slow cooking. When cooked, stir in the sugar and grated raw potato.

Sour-Sweet Cabbage

Coolest oven position or electric casserole
Approx. preparation time 6 minutes

Those who like sour-sweet food will enjoy this cabbage hot or cold. It is a good accompaniment to fresh, pickled or cured pork and makes a delicious base to a salad.

For 2 portions allow:

1 oz (25 g) butter	1–2 tsp. (5–10 ml) sugar
½ lb (200 g) white cabbage, shredded	1 clove
	1 tbs. (15 ml) vinegar
1 small apple, peeled, cored and chopped	salt and pepper to taste

Melt the butter over gentle heat in a flame-proof casserole or a pan with a tightly fitting lid. Add the cabbage, cover and cook till it becomes limp. Remove from heat, and when using a pan, transfer to a casserole (oven or electric). Add the other ingredients, mix well, cover and cook during the day or night as convenient.

Mushrooms

Medium or cool oven position
Preparation time a few minutes

Slowly cooked mushrooms are not only delicious but useful to those who do not shop every day. They keep and reheat remarkably well, and with their tasty liquor, provide a welcome addition to an assortment of dishes.

Clean mushrooms by dipping caps in boiling water and rubbing off any dirt or grit. Remove and slice stalks. Place these and the caps in a casserole. Add a knob of butter, salt and pepper. Cover and cook by day or night.

'Boiled' Potatoes

Oven position depends on variety of potato
Preparation time a few minutes

This recipe is intended for those with no pressure cooker, as, in my opinion, potatoes that have been pressure-cooked are nicer than those that have been boiled, steamed or slow-cooked.

Place scrubbed, unpeeled potatoes in a pan. Cover with boiling water. Add salt. Boil rapidly for a minute. Cover and immediately place in the oven – floury, old potatoes need the coolest position, new or waxy potatoes a medium or hot oven position. When cooked, boil again for about a minute – longer if the potatoes are a little hard. Strain without delay. Either peel the hot potatoes for serving or store unpeeled in a perforated container. The potatoes can be kept a day or so;

stored by this method they can then be fried as potato Lyonnaise, or used in any recipe requiring pre-cooked potato.

Creamed Potatoes

(Cook as soon as prepared)
Coolest oven position
Preparation time a few minutes
  Potatoes cooked this way are good and worth trying whether or not you have a pressure cooker.

Potatoes, peeled and cut into very thin slices	*salt and pepper to taste*
	milk
a little grated onion (optional)	*butter or margarine*

Put the potato, onion and seasoning in a flame-proof casserole or pan with a tightly fitting lid. Just cover with milk. Add a good pat of butter, so that when melted, it forms a layer over the other ingredients. Bring to the boil over gentle heat. Cover and immediately place in the oven.

When cooked, the top potato may be slightly discoloured, but this will not matter once the mixture is mashed and well beaten with a fork.

Baked Creamed Potatoes

This dish is made with cooked *Creamed Potatoes*. Pack some creamed potatoes into a shallow oven dish while still hot and bake and brown in a hot oven, as required.

Pulses

Hot to medium oven position; or electric casserole (*high*, 3 hours)
Preparation time 1 minute

All pulses respond well to ultra-slow cooking.

Haricot beans require soaking in cold water for about twelve hours before cooking. Butter beans, split peas and lentils only need washing.

Put the pulses in a flame-proof casserole or stewpan. Cover well with boiling water. Add salt, and to haricot and butter beans, a little bicarbonate of soda (¼ tsp. 1·25 ml) to a pint (500 ml) of water at most). Place utensil over heat until the water bubbles, cover and immediately place in the oven or transfer to a heated electric casserole.

Sweets and Puddings

Milk Puddings

Hottest oven position or electric casserole
Approx. preparation time 2 minutes
For 2 portions allow:

1 oz (25 g) Carolina rice, or a
  fraction less sago or tapioca
½ pt (250 ml) milk
a small knob butter

2–4 tsp. (10–20 ml) sugar
¼ tsp. (1·25) vanilla or a little
  lemon or orange rind or
  grated nutmeg

Put ingredients in a covered oven dish and place in oven,
or, if using an electric casserole, put ingredients in a pan,
bring to boil and transfer to casserole. Serve hot or cold. Rice
is particularly good cold.

Chocolate or Lemon Rice

Mix either *Chocolate Sauce* (page 150) or *Lemon Curd*
(page 138) into a hot, freshly cooked rice pudding.

Baked Custard

(Cook as soon as prepared)
Hot or medium oven position; or electric casserole (*high*,
  1½–2 hours)
Approx. preparation time 2 minutes

For 2 portions allow:

½ pt (250ml) milk   2 eggs
2 tsp. (10 ml) sugar

Heat milk. Add the sugar and break in the eggs. Whisk well. Pour into a buttered oven dish. Cook in oven (covered with buttered paper) or in an electric casserole. For latter, see section on baking, page 24.

Caramel Custard

(Cook as soon as prepared)
Hot or medium oven position or electric casserole (*high, 1½–2 hours*)
Approx. preparation time:
    2 minutes *Caramel 1*
    8 minutes *Caramel 2*
There is a choice of caramels:

Caramel 1

This may lack the nice burnt taste, but the flavour is good, and it is much simpler to prepare. Place a layer of really dark moist sugar – Barbados if available – on the bottom of a small, not too shallow oven or soufflé dish.

Caramel 2

This is the easiest method of making a real caramel:

4 tbs. (60 ml) each granulated sugar and water

Heat the sugar in a small, really heavy pan over steady heat. Stir now and then so that the sugar discolours evenly. When it has become a very dark brown, add the water a little at a time. Bring to the boil again and boil until syrupy. Pour into a small, not too shallow oven or soufflé dish. Tip it and rotate it so that the bottom and sides are covered with caramel.

Prepare the custard as for *Baked Custard* (page 106). A little vanilla may be added and the sugar may be omitted, according to taste. Pour custard over *Caramel* 1 or 2. Cook in oven (covered with buttered paper) or in an electric casserole. For latter, see section on baking, page 24.

Serve hot or cold. Turn out just before serving.

Chocolate Coffee Cream

(Cook as soon as prepared)

Hot or medium oven position; or electric casserole (*high,* 1½–2 hours)

Approx. preparation time 3 minutes

A delicious sweet for all occasions.

For 4 portions allow :

2 tbs. (30 ml) sugar	4 fl. oz (100 ml) strong coffee
2 tbs. (30 ml) grated chocolate	(instant coffee is satisfactory)
or chocolate powder	12 fl. oz (300 ml) milk
a pinch of salt	3 eggs

Put the sugar, chocolate and salt in a basin and stir in the coffee. Warm the milk, break in the eggs and whisk well. Pour the egg and milk mixture into the chocolate mixture. Whisk again. Transfer to a lightly greased oven dish and cook in oven or an electric casserole. For latter, see section on baking, page 24.

This sweet can be served hot, but is better cold, especially when topped with whipped cream.

Soft Custard

(Cook as soon as prepared)

Medium or cool oven position; or electric casserole (*high,* 1½–2 hours)

Approx. preparation time 2 minutes

Custard powder is so popular because it is foolproof and easy to prepare. This real egg custard is equally foolproof, quicker to prepare and tastes better too. When stacking an ultra-slow oven try to find space for one of these custards. For just under ½ pt (250 ml) custard allow:

1 egg yolk	½" (1 cm) vanilla pod or a
7½ fl. oz (187·5 ml) milk	little vanilla or almond
1–2 tsp. (5–10 ml) sugar	essence

Put the egg yolk in a small basin (plastic or enamel for casserole). Heat the milk and sugar in a small pan until the sugar dissolves. Pour this over the egg and whisk well. Add the vanilla pod – the essences are added to the cooked custard. Cook in oven (covered with lid or foil) or in an electric casserole. For latter, see section on baking, page 24.

The custard must not be stirred during the cooking.

Trifle

A perfect trifle is achieved with a soft egg custard. Soak sponge cakes with sherry or a mixture of sherry and brandy, and spread with raspberry jam or strained, tinned fruit salad. Leave to soak while the soft egg custard is cooking during either the day or night. A little hot milk poured first on the sponges will save on alcohol. It tastes less good, but it is more economical.

When the custard is cooked, pour it, still hot, over the well-soaked sponge cakes.

When cold, top with plenty of whipped cream and garnish with glacé cherries and blanched almonds.

Stewed Fruits

See page 14. Apples are delicious cooked with a little jam.

Fruit Fools

These can be made with any stewed fruit and *Soft Custard* (page 108).

Sieve the fruit as soon as it is cooked and stir in the custard, which may have been cooked at the same time as the fruit or may be cold. Allow about 1 custard to 4 fruit. Serve cold.

Summer Pudding

Medium or cool oven position or electric casserole
Approx. preparation time 5 minutes

This established favourite lends itself well to slow cooking. Unlike the orthodox version, it is made in one operation. Allow:

butter or margarine	*any stewing fruit or rhubarb*
sugar	*a little water, except with*
thin slices of crustless bread	*raspberries and redcurrants*

Grease a basin or soufflé dish and sprinkle lavishly with sugar. Line this with buttered and sugared bread, placing the buttered side towards the basin. Pack firmly with fruit and plenty of sugar. Add the water if necessary. Place buttered sugared bread on top of the fruit and press it down with metal spoon or similar object. Cover with a well-fitting plate or foil. Cook as convenient. For electric casserole, see section on baking, page 24.

When cooked, again press the top bread into the fruit. Turn out when cold. Serve with cream or *Soft Custard* (page 108).

Fruit Meringue Pie

(Cook as soon as prepared)
Hot or medium oven position
Approx. preparation time 8 minutes

This is a delicious way to use egg whites excluded from another dish.

Allow:

fresh fruit or rhubarb (avoid soft fruits other than gooseberries)	sugar to taste

For the meringue: 2 oz (50 g) of caster sugar for each egg white.

Place the sweetened fruit in a greased oven dish. Whisk the egg whites stiffly, then gradually whisk in half the sugar; fold in the remainder. Pile the meringue mixture on top of the fruit, making sure the fruit is completely covered. Place pie in oven.

Serve hot or cold. Topped with whipped cream it makes a wonderful sweet.

Fruit Crumble

Hottest oven position
Approx. preparation time 6 minutes

Any stewing fruit, or rhubarb, sweetened to taste, can be used for this excellent sweet.

For a crumble to cover 2–3 portions of fruit allow:

2½ oz (62.5 g) flour	2 tbs. (30 ml) demerara sugar
1½ oz (37.5 g) butter or margarine	or syrup
	2 tbs. (30 ml) rolled oats

Place the fruit in an oven dish, together with sugar or syrup. Put the flour in a mixing bowl and rub in the fat. Add the brown sugar and rolled oats. Mix well. Sprinkle the crumble evenly over the fruit, making sure the latter is completely covered, and put the dish into the oven.

Serve hot or cold, with cream or *Soft Custard* (page 108).

Stewed Dried Fruits

See page 14.

Stewed Prunes

These are good when cooked in cold tea.

Apricot Fiesta

(Must be prepared at least 12 hours before cooking)
Hottest oven position or electric casserole
Approx. preparation time 5 minutes

This is a really delicious sweet. When made with water,
it is cheap enough for everyday eating, but when made with
sherry (cheapest British sherry is quite adequate) and topped
with cream, it becomes a dish that will grace any party.
For 3–4 portions allow:

5 oz (125 g) dried apricots,
  finely chopped
2½ tbs. (37.5 ml) sago
either 7 fl. oz (175 ml) sherry
  and 8 fl. oz (200 ml) water, or
  17½ fl. oz (437.5 ml) water

4 tbs. (60 ml) sugar, when
  using sherry – 6 when using
  only water
1 egg white (optional)

Place all the ingredients except the egg white in a container. Soak for at least 12 hours. Bring to the boil and cook,
either in a well-covered dish in the oven or in a heated electric
casserole.

When cooked, mix well and, if very solid, add a little more
liquid. Whisk the egg white until stiff and fold it into the
apricot mixture. Pour into individual sundae glasses or fruit
bowls. Serve cold, topped with whipped cream or *Soft Custard*
(page 108), decorated with glacé cherries and blanched
almonds.

Apricot Fiesta can also be used as a filling for *Crunchy Flan Cases* (page 122).

Fig Fiesta

(Must be prepared at least 12 hours before cooking)
Hottest oven position or electric casserole
Approx. preparation time 2 minutes

This, like *Apricot Fiesta*, is a delicious sweet and very economical when made with water. Made with wine it has an unusual subtle flavour – well worth trying for special occasions.

For 3–4 portions allow:

4 oz (100 g) dried figs
4 tbs. (60 ml) sugar
4 tbs. (60 ml) sago
7½ fl. oz (187·5 ml) each of red
 wine and water or ¾ pt
 (375 ml) water

and rind and juice of ½
 lemon
1 egg white (optional)

Chop the figs very finely, and discard stalks. When using water only, crush the lemon rind with a little of the sugar. Proceed as for *Apricot Fiesta* (page 112).

Grape Whip

Hot or medium oven position or electric casserole
Approx. preparation time 15 minutes

An unusual sweet which is popular with children.

For 4–6 portions allow:

1 lb (400 g) white grapes
a small pinch of bicarbonate of
 soda
1–2 tbs. (15–30 ml) brown
 sugar
1 tbs. (15 ml) honey

1 tbs. (15 ml) lemon juice, fresh
 or bottled
2 rounded tbs. (35 ml) sago
cochineal
1 or 2 egg whites

Halve the grapes (skinning unnecessary). Remove pips. Put grapes in a measure. Add water to make up to 1 pt (500 ml). Add bicarbonate of soda, sugar, honey, lemon juice and sago. Stir. Either cook in oven in a small well-covered dish or bring mixture to the boil before cooking in an electric casserole.

When cooked, stir in a few drops of cochineal. Whisk the egg white stiffly and fold it in to the grape mixture while still warm but beginning to set. Turn the whip into a serving dish or individual glasses. Chill. Top with whipped cream or *Soft Custard* (page 108).

Orange Whip

Hot or medium oven position or electric casserole
Approx. preparation time 10 minutes

Like *Grape Whip* (page 113), this is an excellent sweet, a little quicker to prepare and more economical.
For 4–6 portions allow:

1 lb (400 g) oranges, rather more than less	2 rounded tbs. (35 ml) sago
water	1 tbs. (15 ml) sherry (optional)
3 tbs. (45 ml) sugar	1 or 2 egg whites

Peel oranges and remove all the pith. Slice fruit horizontally, discarding pips. Cut up the slices and place them, together with any juice, into a measure and make up to 1 pt (500 ml) with water. Transfer orange and water to a small casserole. Add sugar and sago. Stir. Either transfer to a small, covered dish and cook in the oven or bring to the boil before cooking in an electric casserole.

When cooked, stir well and add the sherry. A little extra orange juice can be introduced if the mixture seems too firm. Whisk the egg white stiffly and proceed as for *Grape Whip*.

Sago Fruit Mould

Hot or medium oven position or electric casserole
Approx. preparation time 2 minutes
For 2–3 portions allow:

¾ pt (375 ml) milk
1½ oz (37.5 g) sago
1½ oz (37.5 g) sugar

a little grated orange or lemon
  peel, crushed with 2 tsp.
  (10 ml) of the sugar
a small tin of fruit other than
  berries

Slow cook all the ingredients, except the tinned fruit, either in a well-covered dish in the oven or bring to the boil and cook in an electric casserole. Before sago is cooked, strain off about half the fruit. Cut it up and stir into the hot, cooked sago. Pour into a wet mould. Chill. Carefully turn out the set mould onto a dish. Garnish with the remaining fruit and pour the syrup over it. This is good served with whipped cream.

Chocolate Cream

Hot or medium oven position or electric casserole
Approx. preparation time 2 minutes
A delightful party dish, easy to prepare, and, without the brandy, a treat for children.
For 4 portions allow:

½ lb (200 g) plain chocolate,
  broken into small pieces
1½ oz (37.5 g) sago

¾ oz (18.75 g) chopped
  walnuts (optional)
16 fl. oz (400 ml) milk
1 tbs. (15 ml) brandy (optional)

Slow cook all ingredients, except the brandy, either in the oven (in a covered, greased container) or in a heated electric casserole, after first bringing to the boil.

When cooked, add the brandy, and stir well. The mixture

should not be too firm : if it is, add a little extra milk or top of milk. Transfer the *Chocolate Cream* to a serving dish or individual sundae glasses. Serve cold. For parties, top with whipped cream and decorate with nuts.

Sultana Pudding

Hot or medium oven position or electric casserole
Approx. preparation time 8 minutes
For 2–3 portions allow :

¼ lb (100 g) bread without crusts	4 tbs. (60 ml) sultanas
½ pt (250 ml) hot milk	2 tbs. (30 ml) caster sugar (can be omitted)
a little rum, kirsch or any other liqueur, or grated lemon or orange rind crushed in sugar, or vanilla essence	2 eggs
	a little butter
	4 tbs. (60 ml) dark moist sugar

Crumble the bread into a basin, and pour the milk over it. Leave until the milk is absorbed and then beat with a fork. Add chosen flavouring, sultanas, sugar and eggs. Beat well. Grease a 6″ (15 cm) pudding basin lightly with butter, put the dark sugar on the bottom. Spoon in the pudding mixture. For oven cooking, cover basin with buttered paper. For cooking in an electric casserole, see section on baking, page 24.

Serve hot or cold. Turn out just before serving.

Viennoise Pudding

Medium or cool oven position or electric casserole
Approx. preparation time 10 minutes
For 4–6 portions allow :

4 oz (100 g) sugar	3 eggs
½ pt (250 ml) milk	3 oz (75 g) sultanas
5 oz (125 g) stale bread, crumbed	2 oz (50 g) mixed peel, chopped
	grated rind of 1 lemon
	small glass of sherry (optional)

Place 2 tbs. (30 ml) of the sugar in a very heavy pan over extremely gentle heat, and, using 2 tbs. (30 ml) water, make a caramel according to directions given for *Caramel 2* (page 107). Add the milk and cook until the caramel is dissolved. Remove from heat. Add the bread and work it in with a fork. Beat in eggs, one by one, and when well blended, stir in remaining ingredients. Transfer mixture to a buttered basin. Lay buttered paper on top for oven cooking. For cooking in an electric casserole, see section on baking, page 24.

Serve hot with a choice of a cold *Hard Sauce* (page 149), hot *Wine Sauce* (page 150), *Soft Custard* (page 108) or cream.

Queen of Puddings

(Cook as soon as prepared)
Medium or cool oven position
Approx. preparation time 8 minutes
    This old favourite can be slow cooked in one operation.
For 2–3 portions allow:

½ pt (250 ml) *milk*	*just over* 1½ oz (37.5 g) *fresh*
½ oz (12.5 g) *butter or*	*breadcrumbs*
margarine	1 *egg*
3 oz (75 g) *caster sugar*	*raspberry jam*

Heat the milk, fat and 1 oz (25 g) of the sugar in a saucepan until the fat has melted. Remove from heat, and stir in the bread. Separate the egg, dropping the yolk into the pan. Stir well and turn mixture into a greased oven dish. Whisk the egg white until very stiff. Whisk in 1 oz (25 g) of the sugar and fold in the remainder. If the bread mixture is still rather wet, leave it a few more minutes before spreading with jam and topping with the meringue. Cook.

Serve hot or cold.

Fruit Queen of Puddings

Prepare and cook as given for *Queen of Puddings* (page 117) with the addition of a layer of strained tinned fruit placed under the jam.

Chocolate Pudding

Hottest oven position or electric casserole
Approx. preparation time 6 minutes
For 3–4 portions allow :

3 rounded tbs. (50 ml) choco- late powder	1 tbs. (15 ml) sugar 1 egg
16 fl. oz (400 ml) milk	½ tsp. (2·5 ml) vanilla
2½ oz (62·5 g) bread, coarsely grated	

Mix the chocolate powder and milk in a small saucepan. Stir over gentle heat until well blended. Add the bread and sugar and cook for 2 minutes. Remove from heat, and place the pan in a bowl of cold water for a minute. Add the egg and vanilla. Beat vigorously with a rotary or wire whisk. Pour the mixture into a well-buttered soufflé dish or pudding basin. For oven, cover with buttered paper; for electric casserole, see section on baking, page 24.

The prepared pudding may be stored in the saucepan. Before cooking a stored pudding give the mixture a final whisk and then transfer it to the greased container.

When cooked, turn pudding out onto a dish. Serve hot or cold with cream or *Soft Custard* (page 108).

Jam Pudding

Hottest oven position or electric casserole
Approx. preparation time 5 minutes

For 3–4 portions allow :

3 oz (75 g) bread, crumbed	2 tsp. (10 ml) water
3 oz (75 g) caster sugar	a pinch baking powder
2 well-beaten eggs	4 tbs. (60 ml) jam – preferably
3 oz (75 g) melted butter	strawberry or raspberry

Mix the bread and sugar in a basin. Stir in the eggs and butter. Heat the water in a small pan, dissolve the baking powder and mix in the jam. Pour this sauce into the bread mixture. Beat well and turn into a thickly buttered soufflé dish, basin or foil container. Cook, covered with buttered paper in oven. For electric casserole, see section on baking, page 24.

When cooked, either turn the hot pudding out onto a warm dish and serve, or store and reheat as required. Serve with *Wine Sauce* (page 150), *Hard Sauce* (page 149), *Soft Custard* (page 108), or jam sauce.

Honey and Ginger Pudding

Hot or medium oven position or electric casserole
Approx. preparation time 5 minutes
For 2–3 portions allow :

5 slices crustless bread	1 egg
2 oz (50 g) crystallized or	2 tsp. (10 ml) sugar
preserved ginger	a pinch of salt
1 oz (25 g) butter or margarine	7½ fl. oz (187·5 ml) milk
1½ tbs. (22·5 ml) honey	1 tbs. (15 ml) water

Cut the bread into cubes. Slice the ginger. Mix them together. Place in a well-greased pie dish. Put the butter and honey in a small pan over gentle heat. Stir with a wooden spoon until blended. Remove pan from heat. Beat in the egg, add the sugar and salt. Gradually stir in the milk and water. Pour this mixture over the bread. Press it down. Cook as convenient in an oven or electric casserole. For latter, see section on baking, page 24.

Serve hot or cold; it reheats well.

Apple Almond Pudding

Hot or medium oven position or large electric casserole
Approx. preparation time 15 minutes

A good party sweet, and not too expensive for everyday menus.

For 5 portions allow:

3½ oz (87.5 g) butter or margarine	1 lb (400 g) cooking apples, peeled, cored and shredded
4 oz (100 g) caster sugar	2 oz (50 g) demerara sugar
1½ oz (37.5 g) ground almonds	2 oz (50 g) breadcrumbs
1 egg	a few chopped blanched almonds

Cream 3 oz (75 g) of the fat with the caster sugar. Beat in the ground almonds and egg with a wire beater until light and fluffy.

Melt the remaining ½ oz (12.5 g) of fat in a shallow 9″ (22 cm) oven dish. Add and mix in the apples, brown sugar and breadcrumbs. Press these evenly into the dish, and cover with the almond mixture. Sprinkle with the chopped almonds. Cook throughout the day or night either in oven or electric casserole. For latter, see section on baking, page 24.

Serve cold, decorated with whipped cream.

Apple Charlotte

Hot or medium oven position or electric casserole
Approx. preparation time 8 minutes

This slow-cooked version of the old favourite is delicious.

For 2 portions allow:

2 oz (50 g) butter or margarine	3 tbs. (45 ml) sugar, preferably
1 medium-sized cooking apple,	demerara
peeled, cored and shredded	a little grated lemon rind and
2 large slices stale bread,	juice or a little cinnamon
coarsely grated	(optional)

Melt the fat in a saucepan and add all the other ingredients. Mix well and transfer to a greased oven dish. Press down firmly. For oven cooking leave dish uncovered. For cooking in an electric casserole, see section on baking, page 24.

Lemon Pudding

(Cook as soon as prepared)
Medium or cool oven position
Approx. preparation time 8 minutes
For 2 portions allow:

2 fairly thick slices stale crust-	2 oz (50 g) caster sugar
less bread	grated rind and juice of 1
a little milk	lemon
2 oz (50 g) softened butter or	2 or 3 eggs
margarine	a little extra sugar

Line a shallow, greased oven dish with fingers of bread. Pour sufficient milk over these to be absorbed by the bread. Cream the fat and sugar. Add the egg yolk and lemon. Beat well. Whisk the whites stiffly, and fold most of this into the creamed mixture and spread it over the soaked bread. Top with the remaining egg white, sprinkle lavishly with sugar and place in the oven.

Serve hot or cold with *Hard Sauce* (page 149) or cream.

Brown Bread Almond Pudding

Hottest oven position or electric casserole
Approx. preparation time 8 minutes

For 3 portions allow :

1 oz (25 g) butter	3 eggs
2 oz (50 g) wholemeal bread- crumbs	2 oz (50 g) sugar
	¼ tsp. (1·25 ml) cinnamon
2½ fl. oz (62·5 ml) red wine or	a little grated lemon rind
1½ tbs. (22·5 ml) lemon juice	1 oz (25 g) ground almonds

Melt the butter in a saucepan and mix in the breadcrumbs.
Add wine or lemon juice and leave a few minutes to get cold.
Beat in the eggs one at a time, then beat in the other ingredients. When the pudding is to be cooked immediately, transfer
the mixture to a well-greased soufflé dish or small cake tin;
otherwise store in the saucepan and give the batter a final
beating just before it goes into the greased container and into
either the oven or an electric casserole. For the latter, see
section on baking, page 24.

When cooked, turn out. Serve with *Soft Custard* (page
108) or *Wine Sauce* (page 150). This pudding reheats well,
but first sprinkle with a little wine or lemon juice and caster
sugar.

Crunchy Flan Cases

Hottest oven position
Approx. preparation time 8 minutes
For 6 small flan cases allow :
Flapjack mixture as given on page 133.

Divide mixture into six. Mould each portion into the
bottom and up the sides of a small greased cake tin. Cook by
day or night, as convenient. Remove from tins when cold.
Suggested fillings : Fresh or tinned fruit topped with whipped
cream.

Cream cheese mixed with preserved ginger
and its syrup.

Apricot Fiesta (page 112) and cream.

Orange Slices (page 144).

Savoury Dishes

Savoury Pie

Medium or cool oven position; or electric casserole (high, 1½–2 hours)
Approx. preparation time 15 minutes
For 2 good portions allow:

3 oz (75 g) fat bacon rashers, cut into pieces
1 large onion, sliced
4 oz (100 g) Cheddar cheese, grated
2 tbs. (30 ml) grated Parmesan (optional but an improvement)

½ pt (250 ml) firmly packed fresh breadcrumbs
2 eggs
1 tsp. (5 ml) French mustard
½ pt (250 ml) milk

Place bacon in a frying pan over gentle heat. Cover and cook until it begins to crispen. Remove bacon from pan and set aside. Put onion in the pan with the fat from the bacon, and fry slowly until it becomes soft. Lift pan from heat. Grease an oven dish, and lay a third of the crumbs on the bottom, then a layer of half the bacon, and a layer of half the onion. Mix the cheeses together, and cover the onion with a third of this mixture. Repeat these layers once more, then a layer of crumbs, and finally top the dish with the remaining cheese. Break the eggs into a small basin, stir in the mustard, add the milk, whisk well and pour over the pie.

Cook as convenient. For electric casserole, see section on baking, page 24.

Serve hot.

Cheese Pudding

Medium or cool oven position, or electric casserole (*high*, 1½–2 hours)

Approx. preparation time 4 minutes

This delicious Boer recipe is rich and should be served with a green salad.

For 2–3 portions allow:

1 egg	6–8 oz (150–200 g) cheese,
1 tsp. (5 ml) made mustard	grated
¼ pt (125 ml) milk	salt to taste
½ oz (12.5 g) oiled butter	a pinch cayenne pepper

Beat the egg in a greased oven dish. Add other ingredients and mix thoroughly. Cook in oven (uncovered) or in electric casserole. For latter, see section on baking, page 24.

Serve hot. *Cheese Pudding* can be reheated as it is, or when cold can be cut into sections and heated and browned in a non-stick frying pan. It can also be spread on toast and placed under a grill.

Shellfish and Sweet Corn Savoury

(Cook as soon as prepared)

Hot or medium oven position or large electric casserole

Approx. preparation time 3 minutes if fish is shelled

For 4 portions allow :

medium tin of sweet corn	*1 tbs. (15 ml) chopped parsley*
at least ¼ pt (125 ml) prawns	*milk*
or shrimps or crab meat,	*2 eggs*
fresh, frozen or tinned	*salt and pepper to taste*
3 oz (75 g) cheese, grated	*browned breadcrumbs*

Strain the corn and tinned fish over a measure. Put the corn and fish in a greased oven dish with most of the cheese and parsley. Add milk to the liquid in the measure to make up to ½ pt (250 ml). Break the eggs into this, add seasoning, whisk well and pour the mixture over the ingredients in the dish. Cover with crumbs and top with the remaining cheese. Immediately place in the oven or electric casserole. For latter, see section on baking, page 24.

Serve either hot or cold with salad.

Frankfurters and Onion Ragout

This dish is made with frankfurters – fresh or tinned – and Onion Ragout (page 100), either while it is still hot or after storing.

Heat the frankfurters in boiling water or their own brine, cut them into 1″ (2 cm) lengths and mix with the hot onion ragout, or mix cold frankfurters with cold onion ragout before reheating.

Kidneys and Onion Ragout

As given for the above recipe, except that chopped fried or grilled kidneys are substituted for frankfurters.

Eggs à l'Indienne

Medium oven position; or electric casserole (high, 1½–2 hours)

Approx. preparation time 15 minutes
For 2 portions allow:

2 hard-boiled eggs	1 tsp. (5 ml) sugar
¾ oz (18·75 g) butter	½ pt (250 ml) milk
1 onion, sliced	2 raw eggs
2 tsp. (10 ml) curry powder	browned breadcrumbs
½ tsp. (2·5 ml) salt	

While the eggs are boiling, melt ½ oz (12·5 g) of the butter in a flame-proof dish or a small saucepan over gentle heat and cook the onions until soft. Remove from heat. Stir in the curry powder, salt and sugar. When using a pan, transfer the mixture to an oven dish. Mix in sliced hard-boiled eggs. The preparation can be carried out thus far in advance of cooking. Just before cooking, break the raw eggs into the milk, whisk well and stir into the prepared mixture. Cover with a layer of crumbs and dot with the remaining butter. For cooking in an electric casserole, see section on baking, page 24.
Serve hot.

RICE DISHES

Rice can be cooked ultra-slowly but one of the orthodox methods must be used for plain boiled rice. This, when cooked by the Slow Cooking Method, will look as it should but the separate grains will be too soft.

Fried Rice

(Cook as soon as prepared)
Coolest oven position; or electric casserole (*high*, 60–70 minutes)
Approx. preparation time 4 minutes

Fried rice can be used in recipes that stipulate boiled rice.
It is perfect except in colour, which is beige instead of white.
For 2–3 portions allow:

1 tbs. (15 ml) olive oil or melted
   lard
3½ oz (87·5 g) patna rice,
   unwashed

12 fl. oz (300 ml) salted boiling
   water or stock

Heat the fat in a pan or flame-proof casserole with a very
well-fitting lid. Fry the rice until it becomes a pale brown.
Pour in the boiling liquid. Stir. Fasten lid and, while still
boiling, place in the oven or transfer to a heated electric
casserole.

When cooked, either serve, or turn into a colander or
sieve to cool before storing.

To reheat, place rice in a sieve over a pan of boiling water
and cover with a folded cloth.

Rice Balls

(Cook as soon as prepared)
Coolest oven position; or electric casserole (high, 70 minutes)
Approx. preparation time 2 minutes

These make a delicious substitute for potatoes.
For 2 portions allow:

2 oz (50 g) patna rice, washed
   and drained
6 fl. oz (150 ml) boiling salted
   water

½ oz (12·5 g) butter or
   margarine
salt and pepper to taste
browned breadcrumbs

Place rice in a small pan or flame-proof casserole with a
very well-fitting lid. Add boiling water and place over heat
to re-boil. Fasten lid and immediately place in the oven or
transfer to a heated electric casserole.

When cooked, mash with a fork and mix in the butter and

seasoning. While still hot, form mixture into little balls and drop these, one at a time, into a small basin containing crumbs. Shake and bounce each ball until covered with crumbs. Unfried, these keep well in a refrigerator or freezer.

Before serving fry them in *butter or lard* until brown, and drain on absorbent paper.

Rice Borders

Borders for egg, fish or vegetable salads can be made with the cooked *Rice Ball* mixture, except that, instead of butter, *Canadian Mayonnaise* (page 149) is mixed into the hot rice. This is then moulded into the shapes required. Chill before filling with salad.

Risotto

Hot or medium position; or electric casserole (*high*, 60–70 minutes)
Approx. preparation time 8 minutes
For 2 portions allow:

2 oz (50 g) patna rice, washed and drained
½ oz (12·5 g) butter or margarine
1 large onion, sliced

2 or 3 tomatoes, skinned and sliced, or 3 tinned Italian tomatoes
salt and pepper
8 fl. oz (200 ml) water or stock
2 oz (50 g) cheese, grated

Heat the fat over gentle heat in a flame-proof casserole or a saucepan with a very close-fitting lid and with the pan covered, cook the onion until clear. Add the tomatoes and work them into the fat with a wooden spoon. Add the remaining ingredients, except the cheese, and either bring to the boil, cover and immediately place in the oven or heated

electric casserole, or store and bring to the boil just before the
slow cooking.

When cooked, stir in the cheese. Serve very hot. This dish
reheats well.

Spanish Rice

Hot or medium oven position; or electric casserole (*high,
60–70 minutes*)
Approx. preparation time 8 minutes
For 2 portions allow:

1 tbs. (15 ml) olive oil
1 medium onion, sliced
¼ lb (100 g) tomatoes, fresh,
  skinned and sliced or
  strained, tinned and cut
2 oz (50 g) patna rice

1 green pepper, seeded and
  sliced
¼ tsp. (1·25 ml) chilli powder
½ tsp. (2·5 ml) salt
8 fl. oz (200 ml) water

Prepare and cook as given for *Risotto*, but omit the cheese.
Spanish Rice is delicious with fried chipolatas.

Savoury Rice

Hottest oven position or electric casserole
Approx. preparation time 2 minutes
For 2 portions allow:

1 tsp. (5 ml) made mustard
½ pt (250 ml) milk
¼ lb (100 g) cheese, grated
1 oz (25 g) carolina rice

pepper to taste
1 tbs. (15 ml) chopped parsley
  or chives (optional)

Mix the mustard and milk in a small casserole. Add the
other ingredients. Cover and cook in the oven or bring to the
boil before cooking in a heated electric casserole.

Savoury Rice Variations

There are many ways of ringing the changes with savoury rice. Any foods, harmonious with rice and cheese, can be added: some to the ingredients before cooking, others to the cooked dish before reheating. For example: *kidneys, mushrooms, sliced peppers, shrimps, prawns* are all good when cooked with the savoury rice. Frankfurters, minced or chopped cooked meat and poultry left-overs, slices of hard-boiled eggs and tomatoes can be added to the dish before reheating, either mixed with the rice or as a garnish. Alternatively they can be added to the hot freshly cooked rice and returned to the oven for a few minutes before serving.

EGG DISHES THAT COOK IN ONE TO FIVE HOURS

Egg dishes, except custard types, become leathery if given the full 8 hours slow cooking. However they cook perfectly in about 2 hours in a slow oven's hottest position or up to 5 hours in its coolest position, or, in 60–70 minutes in an electric casserole set at *high*. For the latter, see the section on baking, page 24.

Bacon and Egg Crisp

(Do not reheat)
See note above for oven position or electric casserole setting
Approx. preparation time 10 minutes
This dish is delicious hot or cold with salad.
For 4 portions double the given quantities

For 2 portions allow:

2 oz (50 g) fat bacon rashers (sliced No. 4)	2 eggs
1½ tbs. (22·5 ml) chopped parsley	1 oz (25 g) butter or margarine
1 small green pepper, seeded and finely sliced (optional, but good)	8 fl. oz (200 ml) moderately packed fresh breadcrumbs
	2 oz (50 g) cheese, finely grated

For 4 portions use a Swiss roll tin.
For 2 portions use a 7" (18 cm) round sandwich tin.

Cover the bottom of the tin with the bacon, and place over gentle heat. Cook until the bacon begins to crispen, moving it round so that it cooks evenly. Remove tin from heat and allow to cool. Sprinkle on the parsley and cover with a layer of green pepper (if used). Carefully break the eggs on top of the other ingredients so that they lie symmetrically and, in the case of two portions, mark their position with two upright pieces of macaroni resting against the side of the tin so that when the cooked dish is cut between the macaroni, a whole egg will be in each portion. Melt the butter in a small pan. Remove from heat and add the crumbs, stir well, then add the cheese. Stir again and spread the mixture over the eggs, making sure they are completely covered, the yolks in particular. Cook in oven or electric casserole.

Spanish Eggs

(Do not reheat)
See page 130 for oven position or electric casserole setting
Approx. preparation time 5 minutes
For 2 good portions allow:

4 eggs	salt and pepper to taste
¼ pt (125 ml) tinned tomatoes	browned breadcrumbs
¼ lb (100 g) cheese, grated	

Beat the eggs. Cut up the tomatoes and add them and their liquor to the eggs. Stir in three-quarters of the cheese and add seasoning. Pour the mixture into a shallow, greased oven dish. Cover thickly with crumbs and top with the remaining cheese. Cook in oven or electric casserole.

Serve hot.

Alpine Eggs

(Do not reheat)
See page 130 for oven position or electric casserole setting
Preparation time 4 minutes

This savoury is adapted from a Swiss recipe which stipulates Gruyère cheese. Made with Cheddar, the dish is not so rich but easier on the budget, and the flavour, though different, is still good.

For 2 portions allow:

1 oz (25 g) butter	¼ pt (125 ml) thin cream or
6 oz (150 g) cheese	top of milk
4 eggs	a little chopped parsley
pepper and salt to taste	browned breadcrumbs

Grease an oven dish thickly with half the butter. Cover the bottom with 4 oz (100 g) of the cheese, thinly sliced. Break the eggs over the cheese, keeping the yolks whole. Season well. Pour the cream over the eggs and cover with the rest of the cheese, finely grated and mixed with the parsley. Top with a layer of crumbs dotted with the remaining butter. Cook in oven or electric casserole.

Serve hot.

Oven Stopgaps

This section gives a choice of stopgaps to fill the odd spaces so often found when stacking a slow-cooking oven.

However some of the recipes, the jams and preserves in particular, deserve oven room in their own right or to be cooked in an electric casserole.

Flapjacks

Hottest oven position
Approx. preparation time 4 minutes
Allow:

4 oz (100 g) margarine or butter	½ lb (200 g) rolled oats, or 6 oz (150 g) rolled oats and 2 oz (50 g) dessicated coconut
1 oz (25 g) sugar	
2 tbs. (30 ml) syrup	¼ tsp. (1·25 ml) salt
	½ tsp. (2·5 ml) mixed spice (optional)

Place the fat, sugar and syrup in a medium to large saucepan over very gentle heat until the fat has softened, without melting. Remove the pan from the heat, beat the mixture well, and when creamy, stir in the other ingredients. Turn the completely blended mixture into a greased baking tin about 8" (20 cm) square. Press down evenly and smoothly with the help of a pliable knife. Cook by day or night as convenient.

When cooked, and still warm, cut into squares or fingers, but leave these in the tin until quite cold. They will keep crisp for a considerable time when stored in an airtight tin.

This flapjack mixture can also be made into *Crunchy Flan Cases* (page 122).

Meringues

(Cook as soon as prepared)
Medium or cool oven position
Approx. preparation time 6 or 10 minutes for 2 egg whites

The Slow Cooking Method always produces superb meringues.

To each egg white allow : 2 oz (50 g) *caster sugar*

Whisk the egg white until very stiff. Either add the sieved sugar, a teaspoon at a time, while still whisking, until the sugar is incorporated, or whisk in half the sugar, a little at a time, and fold in the balance with a metal spoon. Form the meringues with two metal spoons. Put them on to a baking sheet (either covered with Bakewell or brushed with oil) and place immediately in the oven. Cook throughout the day or night.

When cooked, cool the meringues on a wire tray, then store them in an airtight tin.

Coconut Meringues

(Cook as soon as prepared)
Hot or medium oven position
Approx. preparation time 6 minutes

To make 6–8 meringues allow :

1 egg white	2½ oz (62·5 g) desiccated
3½ oz (87·5 g) caster sugar	coconut
	½ tsp. (2·5 ml) cornflour

Whisk the egg white until very stiff, then, still whisking, gradually incorporate the sugar. Finally fold in the coconut and cornflour. Spoon heaps of the mixture onto a well-oiled baking tin or sheet. Place immediately in the oven and cook throughout the day or night.

When cooked, cool the meringues on a wire tray, and store in a tin – they will keep for months, but are not likely to be given the chance !

Peanut Macaroons

(Cook as soon as prepared)
Medium or cool oven position
Approx. preparation time 15 minutes

These, like *Coconut Meringues*, will keep almost indefinitely.

Allow :

¼ pt (125 ml) roasted peanuts*	½ tsp. (2·5 ml) vanilla essence
(not salted)	1 sheet of rice paper (this can
½ tsp. (1·25 ml) salt	be bought in packets either
1 egg white	at Woolworth or at a
¼ pt (125 ml) demerara sugar	stationer)

* Roast shelled peanuts in a baking tin for 10 to 15 minutes in a moderate oven. When cool, remove the husks. If a hair drier is available and can be plugged in near a window, first rub the nuts with the hands to detach the husks, then hold the tin of nuts out of the window and blow the husks away with the drier. Failing this, rub the nuts in a colander until the unwanted husks drop through the holes. The prepared nuts will keep for months in an airtight tin.

Chop the peanuts or put them through a coarse shredder or mincer. Sprinkle them with the salt. Put the egg white on a large plate and beat with a fork to a very stiff froth. Add the sugar and vanilla gradually while still beating. Lastly fold in the nuts. Lay the rice paper on a baking tin – a 7¼″ x 12″ (18 cm x 30 cm) Swiss roll tin is the right size – spread the mixture on to this and immediately place in the oven to cook throughout the day or night.

When cooked, cut into squares while still warm and place on a wire tray to cool before storing in an airtight tin.

Porridge

Medium or cool oven position or electric casserole
Approx. preparation time 3 minutes

When a family includes porridge enthusiasts, it pays to find time in the evening and space in an all-night oven load or an electric casserole for this porridge.
For 4–6 portions allow:

1 pt (500 ml) boiling water	1 tsp. (5 ml) salt
4 tbs. (60 ml) pin-head oatmeal	

Use a pan or a flame-proof casserole. Sprinkle the oatmeal and salt into boiling water. Boil gently for about 2 minutes, stirring now and then. Cover and immediately place in the oven or transfer to a heated electric casserole.

Breadcrumbs

Any oven position

When space can be found in a slow oven, bake any available stale bread, crusts or spurned toast. Once baked, these can be stored – paper bags will do – until the next time the grater or mincer is in action. Then finely grate or mince the baked bread, and store in an airtight tin.

Melba Toast

Coolest oven position

This is made from a not too fresh sandwich loaf.

Slice the bread as thinly as possible and cut off the crusts. Lay slices, if preferred cut in halves, on a wire cake tray. Room can often be found for it on the oven floor. When baked, cool and store in an airtight tin.

Tomato Sauce

Medium or cool oven position or electric casserole

Approx. preparation time 6 minutes

This is a good all-purpose sauce, which keeps for weeks in an airtight container in the refrigerator. It can be served hot or cold and is useful in recipes, see pages 37, 81, 89, 90. To make over ½ pt (250 ml) of sauce, allow :

½ oz (12.5 g) butter or margarine	½ tsp. (2.5 ml) salt
1 small onion, finely sliced	¼ tsp. (1.25 ml) pepper
½ lb (200 g) tomatoes, skinned and chopped (cooking tomatoes will do)	2–4 tsp. (10–20 ml) sugar, according to taste
	2 tsp. (10 ml) sago
	3 fl. oz (75 ml) water

Fry the onion in a small pan or flame-proof casserole with a tightly fitting lid. When clear but not brown, add the tomatoes and cook for a further 2 minutes, working them into the fat and onions with a wooden spoon. Add the remaining ingredients, and either cook, or store and cook later. In both cases bring sauce to the boil immediately before putting it in the oven or transferring it to a heated electric casserole.

When cooked, the sauce can be used as it is, though if preferred it can be worked through a sieve or strainer while still hot.

Lemon Curd

Coolest oven position or electric casserole (*high*, 2 hours)
Approx. preparation time 15 minutes

An excellent lemon curd – a good oven stopgap when
eggs are cheap, and quick in an electric casserole.

To make just under 1 lb (400 g) of curd allow :

2 oz (50 g) *butter*	*grated rind and juice of 1 large*
6 oz (150 g) *caster sugar*	*lemon*
	1 whole egg and 3 egg yolks

Put the butter, sugar and lemon into a small pan over
gentle heat, and stir with a wooden spoon until the sugar has
dissolved. Remove from heat, and stand the pan in cold water
for a few minutes to cool. Then add the eggs, beating them
into the mixture with a fork. Transfer the curd to a small
well-covered oven container or a Kilner jar. Immediately before cooking whisk with a rotary whisk. Cook as convenient
in oven or electric casserole. For latter, see section on baking,
p. 24.

When cooked, stir well, and either store in container in
which it was cooked or pour into a jar. Cover when cold.

See *Lemon Rice* (page 106).

JAM, MARMALADE AND PRESERVES

JAM

All those who have tried jam-making by the Slow Cooking
Method are most enthusiastic : it is certainly 'jam without
tears'. Quite small quantities can be made, using as little as
½ lb (200 g) of fruit. This is ideal for those with a few fruit
trees or bushes in their garden, also for small families who like
a wide choice of jams. The flavour is superb and the jam sets,
without manufactured aids, in next to no time. There is a
scientific reason for this. The pectin and acid in the fruit

transforms the syrup into a jell and very slow cooking of the fruit without sugar is the best method of extracting pectin and turning fruit acid and pectose into pectin. Thus cooking the fruit with very little liquid and without boiling, produces the maximum pectin with the minimum loss of flavour and colour.

Method for making slow-cooked jams

Cook the fruit and liquid in one or more covered containers in the oven's medium to cool position or in an electric casserole throughout the day or night.

When cooked and still hot, transfer to a large saucepan or preserving pan, add the sugar, also hot, and place over gentle heat. Stir until the sugar has dissolved. Raise the heat and boil rapidly for 2 minutes. Test for jell – the jam may well have set already; if not, it will only need another minute or so.

Apple,* Apricot, Blackcurrant, Cherry, Damson, Gooseberry, Greengage, Loganberry, Peach, Pear,* and Plum Jams

To each lb (400 g) (after preparation) of any of these fruits allow :

¼ pt (125 ml) water or, for special jams,	*wine, sherry or rum* **
	1 lb (400 g) sugar

Strawberry Jam

To each lb (400 g) of strawberries allow :

1 lb (400 g) sugar and 2 oz (50 g) gooseberries slow cooked with 1 tbs. (15 ml) water. Crush strawberries with sugar. Set

---

* Apple jam and pear jam are excellent when crystallized ginger is added. Cook this with the fruit and water allowing at least 2 oz (50g) chopped ginger to each lb (400g) of fruit.

** Alcohol is particularly good with apple.

aside 12 hours before mixing with slow-cooked gooseberries. Boil 2 minutes.

Blackberry Jam

To each lb (400 g) of blackberries allow :

¼ pt (125 ml) water   ¾ lb (300 g) sugar

To eliminate pips, the cooked fruit may be sieved before the sugar is added.

Rhubarb and Orange Jam

To each lb (400 g) of rhubarb allow :

the juice of 1 orange, and   *1 lb (400 g) sugar*
the rind, grated and crushed
with a little sugar (optional)

Dried Apricot Jam

To each lb (400 g) of dried apricots allow :

2 pt (1 litre) water   *2–3 oz (50–75 g) almonds,*
2 lb (800 g) sugar   *blanched and finely sliced*

Cut the washed apricots into small pieces and soak in the water for at least 24 hours before cooking. When cooked, add hot sugar and almonds. Proceed as for other jams.

MARMALADE

When making slow-cooked marmalade, the fruit need not be soaked. Most recipes can be adapted to this method, provided the amount of water is slightly reduced. It is better not to cook the fruit whole, but to slice it as thinly as possible and remove pips before cooking. Use the same method as given for slow-cooked jams, except the prepared fruit must first be warmed in the oven in its container or in an electric casserole at *high*. Boil the required amount of water and pour it over the fruit. Place the covered container immediately in the oven's hottest position or leave the casserole at *high* for 45 minutes before switching to *low*. The cooked fruit and sugar will require longer boiling before it sets. Start testing for jell after 15 minutes rapid boiling, although some oranges and large quantities will need considerably longer.

Seville Marmalade

To make just over 7 lbs (2 kg 800 g) allow:

2 lb (800 g) *Seville oranges*	4 lb (1 kg 600 g) *sugar*
½ *lemon*	½ pt (250 ml) *cold water*
3 pt (1·5 *litres*) *boiling water*	

Heat the finely sliced fruit in one or two containers or an electric casserole. Place pips in a small basin. Pour most of the boiling water over the heated fruit. Cover and immediately cook for at least 8 hours. Reheat remaining water to boiling point and pour this over the pips. Cover basin and set aside.

When the fruit is cooked and the sugar is heating, tip the pips and liquor into a small pan and bring to the boil. After a minute, strain liquid into the fruit and boil pips again with ¼ pt (125 ml) water. Strain into the fruit and repeat operation with the final ¼ pt (125 ml) water.

The following recipes are useful when Seville oranges are not available.

Sweet Orange Marmalade

To make about 4 lbs (1 kg 600 g) allow:

2 lb (800 g) oranges
1½ pt (750 ml) boiling water

2 lb (800 g) sugar
2 tsp. (10 ml) tartaric acid

Sweet Orange and Grapefruit Marmalade

To make about 7 lbs (2 kg 800 g) allow:

2 oranges
1 lemon
1 medium grapefruit

3 pt (1·5 litres) boiling water
5 lb (2 kg) sugar

Grapefruit Marmalade

To make about 3 lbs (1·5 kg) allow:

1 lb (400 g) grapefruit
1 pt 12 fl. oz (800 ml) boiling
  water

1 lb 12 oz (700 g) sugar

PRESERVES

Slow-cooked preserves are as successful as slow-cooked jams.
They need a far shorter final boil than is demanded by the
recipes from which they are adapted, but considerably longer
than the jams.

Quince Preserve

Nowadays quinces are not always easy to get. Anyone
who practises the Slow Cooking Method should snap up
2 lbs (800 g) or more on sight, and make this preserve – it's
delicious.

Wipe the fruit. Place in one or more oven containers or a heated electric casserole. Cover completely with boiling water. Close lids. Immediately cook for at least 8 hours in a medium to cool oven position. If using an electric casserole set on *high* for the first ½ hour.

When cooked, strain the liquid into a saucepan. Peel or scrape, quarter and core the quinces as soon as they are cool enough to handle. Add the skin and cores to the liquid and boil rapidly until the quantity is reduced to between ⅓ and ½, and the colour has changed to a yellowish pink. While the liquid is boiling, weigh the quinces and heat the same weight of sugar in the cool oven. Slice the quartered quinces into small pieces or pass them through a coarse shredder. When the liquid has boiled sufficiently, strain the liquor into a large saucepan or preserving pan. Place over gentle heat. Add the quince and hot sugar. Stir until the sugar has dissolved. Boil for 6 to 20 minutes before testing for jell, depending on the ripeness of quinces.

Marrow Preserve

This preserve does require about 50 minutes boiling, which is certainly better than the 4 hours stipulated in the original recipe. Anyhow, the time should not be grudged, as the result is so good.

To each 2 lbs (800 g) marrow after removal of skin, pulp and pips allow:

2 lb (800 g) *sugar*
2 oz (50 g) *crystallized or preserved ginger, cut up*
3 oz (75 g) *strained tinned pineapple, cut up*

grated rind and juice of ½ lemon
a small pinch of cayenne

Cut the marrow into strips or small cubes and place in a bowl with the other ingredients. Leave for 12 hours. Then tip the mixture into a pan over heat. Stir until the sugar dissolves. When it begins to boil, either transfer to one or more hot oven containers with close-fitting lids and immediately place in the oven's hottest position, or, tip boiling fruit into heated electric casserole. Cook about 8 hours leaving casserole on *high* for the first ½ hour.

After this slow cooking pour the hot mixture back into the pan. Place over low heat and boil very gently for about 50 minutes before testing for jell.

Pickled Pears

A delicious pickle to serve with cold meat or as a sambal with curried chicken (page 60). The pears should not be too ripe; wind-falls will do.

To make about 5 lbs (2·5 kg) allow :

¼ pt (125 ml) *white wine* *vinegar*	2 oz (50 g) *crushed root ginger* ½ tsp. (2·5 ml) *cloves*
rind and juice ½ *lemon*	3½ lbs (1·75 kg) *pears, peeled,*
1¾ lb (700 g) *sugar*	*cored and sliced*

Place vinegar, lemon and sugar in a flame-proof casserole or saucepan over heat. Stir until the sugar dissolves; then boil for a few minutes. Add ginger and cloves (tied in a bag). Boil a further few minutes. Add the pears. If applicable, transfer to an oven dish with a well-fitting lid, or an electric casserole. Slow cook until the pears are clear. Remove bag. Spoon pears and syrup into hot screw-topped jars.

Orange Slices

(Cooked in two slow-cooking sessions)

This delicious preserve may not keep as well as jam – but, once introduced, its days will be numbered. The slices can be served in tartlet cases or as garnishes for cold or hot sweets.

Stage 1. Hottest oven position or electric casserole
Approx. preparation time 5 minutes
For 4 oranges

Grate off the surface rind and place oranges in a container with a well-fitting lid or an electric casserole. Completely cover the fruit with boiling water and immediately slow cook until tender.

When cooked, strain the oranges and store until the next slow-cooking session.

Stage 2. Hottest oven position or electric casserole
Approx. preparation time 8 minutes
Allow:

the 4 oranges cooked in Stage 1	½ pt (250 ml) water
12 oz (300 g) sugar	2 tbs. (30 ml) lemon juice (fresh or bottled)

Cut the oranges into ¼″ (0·5 cm) slices and remove the pips. Dissolve the sugar in the liquid. Place the orange slices and juice in a container with a well-fitting lid or heated electric casserole. Boil up the syrup and pour it over the fruit. Slow cook immediately until transparent.

When cooked, carefully lift the slices into heated jam or screw-topped jars – not too many in a jar. Boil the syrup to reduce quantity, leaving sufficient to fill the jars and completely cover the fruit. Cover the jars when cold.

Apple Chutney

An excellent chutney and a good way of using windfalls.
To each lb (800 g) of prepared apples allow:

1–2 oz (25–50 g) sultanas
⅛–¼ oz (3–6 g) ground ginger
1 oz (25 g) grated onion
¼–½ clove garlic
    crushed in salt

1 chilli, 1 clove, 4 peppercorns
    and 4 mustard seeds (spices
    tied up in a piece of muslin)
3 fl. oz (75 ml) vinegar
3 oz (75 g) dark moist sugar
¼–½ oz (6–12 g) salt

Place the apple, sultanas, ginger, onion, garlic, spices and
vinegar in a covered container in a cool or medium oven
position or in a heated electric casserole. Transfer cooked mixture to a large saucepan or preserving pan and add the pre-
viously heated sugar and salt. Place over heat, stir until the
sugar has dissolved, then boil rapidly for a few minutes. Remove spice bag after squeezing it dry. Pour chutney into
pre-heated jars.

Slow Cooking Supplements

Very slow and very quick cooking are complementary. When both methods are used, the most varied and interesting meals are produced with the least effort and preparation time.

The pressure cooker is an invaluable companion to that established quick-cooking pair – the grill and the frying pan.* It proves its worth for potatoes (page 103), runner and French beans, spinach, sprouts, cauliflower, etc., even if used for no other purpose.

Although recipes for quickly cooked food are not within the scope of this book, the following are included as they are useful accompaniments both to slowly and quickly cooked dishes.

SAUCES

Mustard Sauce

Approx. preparation time 6 minutes

This sauce, so quick and simple to prepare, keeps for weeks in a refrigerator and is delicious with bacon, ham, fish and salads. As it does not mind an ultra-slow oven, it can be used

---

* Whenever possible, use a non-stick frying pan. Of these, Colorcast are most satisfactory and do not need as much attention as many other makes.

in slowly cooked recipes, e.g. *Fish in Mustard Sauce*, page 37, *Gammon Rasher Cooked in Sauce*, page 89.

2 hard-boiled eggs	2 tbs. (30 ml) vinegar (garlic
2 tbs. (30 ml) olive oil	vinegar if available)
4 tsp. (20 ml) German or	1 tbs. (15 ml) chopped parsley
French mustard	1 tbs. (15 ml) grated onion
1 tbs. (15 ml) sugar	2 tsp. (10 ml) chopped chives
¼ tsp. (1·25 ml) salt	or other green herbs
a little freshly milled pepper	

Place the egg yolks in a small basin and crush them with a wooden spoon. Gradually stir in the oil, to make a smooth paste. Add the mustard, sugar and seasoning, and, still stirring, gradually incorporate the vinegar. An electric liquidizer will blend the egg yolks, oil, mustard, sugar, seasoning and vinegar in one operation. Chop the egg whites very finely. Add these, the parsley, onions and herbs. Store the sauce in a covered refrigerator container.

Horseradish Sauce

This is made with the above mustard sauce and Heinz's dried horseradish.*

Allow :

1 tsp. (5 ml) dried horseradish	4 tsp. (20 ml) mustard sauce
1½ tsp. (7·5 ml) milk	

Mix the horseradish and milk. Cover and let stand for at least 10 minutes before adding the mustard sauce.

* Dried horseradish is one of the 57 varieties, but sometimes difficult to find – however, retailers should be able to produce it when requested.

Canadian Mayonnaise

Approx. preparation time 6 minutes

This easy-to-make mayonnaise is not as rich as orthodox mayonnaise and has the advantage of not objecting to slow cooking, see *Salmon Mayonnaise and Fish Salad*, page 38.

2 egg yolks	4 fl. oz (100 ml) vinegar or
1 tsp. (5 ml) salt	lemon juice (fresh or bottled)
¼ tsp. (1·25 ml) pepper	1 oz (25 g) margarine
1 tsp. (5 ml) dry mustard	2½ tbs. (22·5 ml) plain flour
1 tbs. (15 ml) sugar (optional)	8 fl. oz (100 ml) warm water
4 fl. oz (100 ml) olive oil	

Put the yolks, seasonings, oil, vinegar or lemon in a mixing bowl. Melt the margarine in a saucepan. Stir in the flour, and when smooth, gradually add the water. Place over medium heat, and stir until the mixture thickens and boils. Immediately pour the hot sauce over the other ingredients and whisk the lot together with a rotary whisk. In a matter of moments a creamy mayonnaise is produced. When cold, pour into a jar. It keeps well for months in a refrigerator.

Sauce Tartare
See page 38.

Tomato Sauce
See page 137.

Hard Sauce

Approx. preparation time 3 minutes

2 oz (50 g) warmed unsalted butter	2 tsp. (10 ml) either lemon juice, brandy or rum
2 oz (50 g) caster sugar	1 stiffly whisked egg white (optional)

Liquidize the first three ingredients or cream the butter in a small basin with a wooden spoon. Gradually beat in the sugar and chosen liquid. Lastly, using a metal spoon, fold in the egg white. Chill and store sauce in a refrigerator or freezer. It is good served with hot puddings.

Wine Sauce

Approx. preparation time 5 minutes

This delicious sauce is served hot. It can be stored in a refrigerator for some time and reheated as required.

1 oz (25 g) butter	1 oz (25 g) sugar
½ oz (12·5 g) flour	2½ fl. oz (62·5 ml) sherry
7½ fl. oz (187·5 ml) water	

Melt the butter in a small saucepan and stir in the flour. Then add the water and stir until the mixture boils. Cook for two or three minutes. Remove from heat and stir in the sugar and sherry.

Chocolate Sauce

Approx. preparation time 3 minutes

This very popular sauce is quick to prepare and keeps well in a refrigerator. It is good with ice cream and transforms everyday sweets into something special; see *Chocolate Rice*, page 106.
Allow :

1 oz (25 g) butter or margarine	2½ tbs. (37·5 ml) sugar
2 level tbs. (30 ml) cocoa	¼ tsp. (1·25 ml) vanilla
2 tbs. (30 ml) water	

Put all the ingredients into a small saucepan over gentle heat. Stir until the ingredients are blended, but do not allow to boil. Pour into a refrigerator container.

STUFFINGS

Veal Forcemeat

This is a good all-purpose stuffing.
For 4–6 portions allow:

2 oz (50 g) fresh breadcrumbs
2 oz (50 g) shredded suet (1 oz
  (25 g) only if meat is fatty)
½ tsp. (2·5 ml) salt
¼ tsp. (1·25 ml) pepper
1 tbs. (15 ml) chopped parsley

1 tsp. (5 ml) powdered thyme
½ tsp. (2·5 ml) grated lemon
  rind
a good pinch of nutmeg
beaten egg for binding

Put all the dry ingredients in a basin, mix well and add
sufficient egg to make a manageable stuffing.

Forcemeat Balls

These are made with Veal Forcemeat. They can be prepared in advance but must be fried shortly before serving.
They make a welcome addition to casseroles and soups.

Form the forcemeat into small balls.

Shallow or deep fry in butter, lard or oil until brown all
over.

Economical Stuffing

A good stuffing for boned, rolled breast of lamb, the most
economical of all roasts (page 78).
To stuff a breast of lamb allow:

2 oz (50 g) fresh breadcrumbs
1 medium onion, shredded
1 tbs. (15 ml) chutney or 2
  tbs. (30 ml) shredded apple

salt and pepper
1 oz (25 g) melted margarine
1 tbs. (15 ml) dried mixed
  herbs (optional)

Put all the ingredients in a basin and stir until blended.

Index